FROM MINER

# FROM MINER TO MAJOR

*by*

PETER LAWLESS MSM

The Memoir Club

© Peter Lawless 2010

First published in 2010 by
The Memoir Club
Arya House
Langley Park
Durham
DH7 9XE
Tel: 0191 373 5660
Email: memoirclub@msn.com

British Library Cataloguing in
Publication Data.
A catalogue record for this book
is available from the
British Library

ISBN: 978-1-84104-503-0

Typeset by TW Typesetting, Plymouth, Devon
Printed by J F Print, Sparkford, Somerset

*To Enid, childhood friend,*
*devoted wife and companion.*

# Contents

**Part Three – Civvi Street**

# List of Illustrations

# Acknowledgements

I wish to say that without the assistance and encouragement of Janet Wright, this book would never have been written. I thank her gratefully for her enthusiasm, and for giving me a boot up the backside whenever I faltered in this project. She was certainly my guide and wise counsellor.

I also want to thank my eldest granddaughter Sarah, who first put the idea to me of writing a book about my life and times. Also all the other people who egged me on and all those friends and relations who produced loads of information, particularly of the earliest years, things this old and feeble mind failed to recall until reminded.

I must thank my regiment, The Rifles, for kindly allowing me to reproduce extracts from the *Oxf. & Bucks LI, KRRC, RB & RGJ Chronicle*, In particular Lt. Col. Jan-Dirk von Merveldt who has been most helpful and remained calm and collected despite my persistent and sometime idiotic enquiries.

Many thanks also to the Society of London Golf Captains, the Truants Golf Society and the North Middlesex Golf Club, all of whom accepted me as a member of their organisations and who were most helpful and informative whilst I was carrying out my research. Also Bernie Bristow for helping with the photographic content of the book.

Finally I would like to remember my late wife Enid, who played a *major* part in shaping my life and making it full of fun, and interesting enough for me to feel writing a book about it was worth while. She was constantly in my thoughts as I worked on this autobiography.

# Preface

I'm writing this book not for any personal aggrandisement but purely and simply as a record of my achievements and ambitions throughout my life: things that happened to me, things that didn't happen to me and things I shared with others. I write this autobiography for my grandchildren and their grandchildren, in fact for all the family that will be following on behind. This is so that they, and future generations, can at least remember me in their thoughts and have some idea of the make-up of the old man. If it is also of interest and amusement to other readers then it will all have been worth while.

# Foreword

This is a very readable, honest and personal account of the early years of Major Peter Lawless, his time in the Army and subsequent civilian career. It will be enjoyed by his grandchildren, his many friends and I am sure a wider audience. To begin with we are given an insight into how hard life was during the Second World War in his close knit family. Somehow life did go on, despite the obvious difficulties. As the eldest child Peter displayed early signs of leadership and compassion which would stand him in good stead later on in his chosen career.

A broken leg turned out to be a turning point. Peter could have pursued a career as a professional footballer, but he chose to join the Army. As he puts it: 'I think they would have taken anybody who could breathe at that time'!

What follows is an enjoyable roller coaster ride recounting the ups and downs of Army life in the UK and in a number of overseas postings: Cyprus, Kenya, Borneo, Penang, and Berlin. He recalls how his footballing skills helped him achieve early promotion. The sadness that followed the break up of his family is countered later when he meets and marries Enid who became a life long friend, mother and companion.

I first met Peter Lawless when he was RSM at the Rifle Depot in Winchester. I recall the early morning sword drill sessions hidden (!) behind the drill sheds as if they took place yesterday. As a young officer I remember him as a courteous, helpful but firm senior NCO whom I am glad to say became a good friend.

He fully deserved his subsequent commission and the Regiment, in particular the members of the Royal Green Jackets Territorial Army Battalion (4 RGJ), will always be grateful for the huge amount of work that he did at Davies Street and in the London Club. I was proud to be one of his Commanding Officers.

Throughout this book, of remarkably detailed recollections, shines his infectious and cheeky sense of humour. He always seemed to see the slightly bizarre and amusing side of events. The book is written in a 'down to earth' way that many of his colleagues will enjoy. Enid would probably have been embarrassed had she lived to read it. However, his grandchildren and friends will treasure this account, and so will many other people who did not know this charming, thoughtful and decent family man.

Brigadier (Retd) Peter Lyddon MBE (late RGJ)
August 2010

PART 1

# Early Years

# CHAPTER 1

# Earliest years

I WAS BORN AT A VERY early age. I was nought when I was born, and it took me twelve months to become one, by which time my mother was heavily pregnant with her second son, I being the first. In fact, my mother produced five children within six years.

As the eldest I think I was favoured. Once when Mother was bathing me in the tin tub before the hearth, my father was heard to say, 'You know, Mona, when this lad grows up, he's going to go down big with the girls, particularly if you keep lifting him out of the bath like that.' Mother learned the proper way; none of my other brothers profited.

Father, Walter, was a miner and also a devout Catholic which meant we kids hardly ever saw him because he was working throughout the week and on Sunday he was at church. My mother Mona (née Foulkes) was semi-converted, although she hardly ever went to church. I was conceived in 1929 but not born until 1930. My parents were married in August 1929 and I was born on 16 January 1930. Hence I just avoided being a 'right little bastard', as I was often referred to in later years when I became a Regimental Sergeant Major (RSM) but more of that later.

As I said, I was the first of five children. My birth was followed thirteen and half months later by Walter, then another fourteen months after that by Mona Maria – the only girl, who could never work out how it was that she had four brothers and I only had three. Next came my second brother, Harry (Patrick Henry), who was born sixteen months after Mona. Jim (James Keith), my youngest brother, followed two years and eight months after Harry. I think that by this time Mother had found out what was causing the births. Anyway we never had any more.

My brother Walter and I, as we were growing up, used to complain that we had only one Christian name whilst the others had two. Mum said, 'When you two were born we were very poor, and could only afford one name; you had to pay the registrar extra for each name.' I never believed a word of it.

Thus we were a family and lived at 18 Brickfield Row, Holmes, Rotherham in South Yorkshire. Life was fairly good despite being impoverished. But for being poor, we certainly were that. I was lucky, for being the eldest I got the new clothes – which wasn't often – and my clothes were handed down to Walter and so on, as long as they lasted. Shoes were always a problem. At one stage Walter and I wore clogs. Shoes always needed mending, for they were worn until the soles wore out, and then had cardboard from Quaker Oats boxes, shaped and put in the shoe, to avoid taking them to the cobbler's. Money was seriously tight.

Although a large family in a small house, with little difference between our ages, we got on well with each other. We had one or two fall-outs but generally had lots of fun so, poor as we were, we were happy enough; we had to be, after all we didn't know any different. We ate what we were given, which wasn't always enough but that's how things were in those early days. Crockery was our biggest problem; it was being broken so often that eventually we were reduced to drinking from jam jars.

Our house was a two up, two down, terraced house on a road that was unadopted which meant that it had no Tarmac surface. The pavement was made up of upended house bricks held in place by concrete slabs: not very pretty but they did the job. Trade vehicles, lorries and vans, hardly ever came down the street and nobody in our district owned a car. Occasionally the knife-grinder with his bicycle and sometimes the pikelet man ventured down but the ice-cream man with his vehicle stayed at the end of the street playing his music. Another regular chap who came on his bike was the fellow who put out the gas lamps; I remember that he had a long pole with a hook on the end. There was another guy who came infrequently who was a German Jew who carried a knapsack on his back with panes of glass of all different sizes, shouting, 'You vant new vindows?'; he couldn't sound his w's. We children used to mock him by shouting after him, 'Got any *vindows?*'

There was also the rent man, who was not always welcome. This was because on the odd occasion Mum had used the rent money for something that she felt was more important and therefore couldn't pay. She would make us kids all sit quietly on the settee like the three wise monkeys and pretend that nobody was home – this was spoilt the first time by me shouting out, 'We're not in!' Our situation was no different from anyone else in our area and I'm sure the rent man knew this. As we always paid up in the end, this didn't cause any major problems.

In Rotherham we lived in constant smog which wasn't all from people's chimneys but mainly from the grime and soot from local factories. I remember one incident when I was about four years old. I'd been out playing and when I came home I saw a man peering in the window. I said to Mum, 'There's a man looking in our front window.' Mum took a look and replied, 'You silly lad, it's Mr Charlesworth, he's reading our curtains.' You see, Mum only had one set of net curtains and so when they came down to be washed (which was three or four times a week because of all the smog) she put up sheets of newspaper to stop people outside from seeing in. It couldn't have been a very healthy period but we all seemed to have survived OK. As I write this all four of my siblings are alive and well and they're all in their seventies.[1]

The houses were all on one side of the road, facing open fields. These fields were unattended and overgrown but with paths beaten through them that people had made passing from their street to ours and beyond. We kids had many happy hours making cricket pitches on those paths.

We didn't have electricity in the house until just before the Second World War started. Our oven was by the side of the open fire in the living room. As Dad worked down the pit we had plenty of coal, so much so that Mum would sometimes sell the odd bucketful to supplement the housekeeping. The fire provided all our hot water, heating the pans and kettles constantly on the hob. It heated the oven, the hand irons and the house bricks we used as bed warmers. The kitchen also had a built-in copper with a fire under it and housed the washing tubs with scrubbing board, poncher or dolly and standing mangle.

In the living room, ironically, we had an upright piano. Looking back, it's curious that although we were very poor, with no money, living off scraps, with Mum scrimping and scraping to keep us decently dressed, we had a piano. However it did provide us with great fun and entertainment. Most Sunday evenings we would have a sing-song around it with our near-by relatives and neighbours joining in. Still, it's a mystery how we came by it, considering that we were living in a house where furniture was at a premium. We only had six chairs to seat five kids and two adults – we did have a sofa of sorts but that, the piano and the dining table, sideboard, and chairs were all in the same room that we lived in. You could say that we were a very close family; almost touching.

Sleeping was not too clever and as the family kept increasing, things got worse. Finally we ended up with sister Mona sleeping in our parents' room,

[1]Since finishing the book, and before printing, I'm saddened to say that my brother Walter had a severe stoke from which he failed to recover, and died in Rotherham and District Hospital, early in 2010.

and we four boys in the other bedroom in a big double bed, 'top and tail' as we used to say. We used to talk for a bit but we did eventually get to sleep. We had our hot bricks for water bottles and our 'po' or potty under the bed. However one of us – no names, no pack drill – was a bed wetter. I think this was why we all learned to swim very quickly and as I was eldest I slept in the shallow end. The potty was necessary as we only had an outside toilet across the yard and no one ventured out at night, particularly during the cold frosty winters. Before we had electricity we went to bed with a candle. Mum would leave us to settle and then come up and blow it out; we were normally asleep by then.

So life went on, and we got on like a house on fire, or mostly so. By the time the war broke out, four of us had started school. Only our Jim was left at home; he went to infant school about a year later.

CHAPTER 2

# School years and the War

A T THE AGE OF FIVE I went to school like most children did at that time. I went to Ferham Road Infant School[2] and shared a desk with I girl I knew called Enid Paine who, unbeknown to me then, was to become my wife. She knew how to get me into trouble right from the start, telling tales to the teacher that would result in me getting a slap on the leg with a ruler. However I soon got over those things and life went on.

When I was seven I changed schools and started at St Bede's Roman Catholic School with brother Walter; my other brothers and sister all started their school lives at St Bede's. We walked to and from school in a group from our district. Perhaps we did do some things I wouldn't advocate today and occasionally the odd fight broke out when someone did something someone else didn't like but nothing too serious.

My sister Mona seemed to always be able to find trouble and get me involved in it too. On the way to school she would come over and say, 'Pete' – my siblings always called me Pete – 'that lad over there has been hitting me.' So I would go across to him to find out what had been going on only to be told something like 'that little bitch started to kick us and call us names' and I would inevitably end up in a fight. That was Mona (named after my mother) and I think she had Mum's temper too – quick to lose it but equally quickly forgotten!

In the August before the war began we went on a family holiday, the first one we ever had. We went to Withernsea on the east coast of Yorkshire, about twelve to fifteen of us: aunts, uncles and cousins. I mention this because of an incident that occurred one day whilst we were on the beach. The beach was being prepared for any possible German invasion as the war was imminent, so only small areas were available to us kids to build our sandcastles and play. At the end of this particular day, the early evening to be exact, we were preparing to go back to our digs when someone noticed that our Harry was missing. Panic stations ensued and everybody went in different directions searching for him. Then Mother in

---

[2]A long time after me David Seaman the England and Arsenal goalkeeper also went to this school, as did his brother Colin, who in later years became our insurance man.

her innocence said that the Germans had probably sneaked over early and had captured him. The mind boggles at the thought of a crack German snatch squad coming all the way from Germany to get our Harry, aged six. After about three hours searching we returned to the digs where we found Harry on the doorstep. He got a good hiding for causing such a hoo-ha.

A few months into the war Mother started work in a factory as a crane driver – as if she didn't have enough on her plate bringing up five kids. As most of the men had gone off to the war, I suppose she thought she had to, no doubt wanting to do her bit towards the war effort.

Dad used to get up at 5 a.m. to catch the bus to take him to the pit. A knocker-upper would come round before the bus was due to make sure that everyone was up in time to catch it. As the war progressed Dad would often work double shifts; that is to say, he would work the morning shift and stay on to work a second. This was possible because there was a shortage of manpower due to the war. Although mining was a reserved occupation, many preferred to join up rather than work down the pit. However this did give Dad an extra bob or two.

Mum never worked nights, not wanting to leave us kids alone at home all night, but Father sometimes did. However when both parents were working the afternoon shift at the same time, that in effect left me – I was ten years old by this time – as the leader of the pack, so to speak, and responsible for the well-being of my four siblings. This meant ensuring they all got home from school okay, then getting them food and drink and generally taking care of them, as well as getting them to go to bed before my parents got home. Because of the black-out in the evenings we hardly ever went out into the fields or back yard to play, especially in the winter months because without a moon or with overcast skies, it was pitch black. We sometimes had a few mates round after school or maybe went to their house. I was allowed to stay up to report on any problems that might have arisen and generally give an account of our activities since getting home from school. It was usually November – Tango – Romeo (Nothing To Report).

It was difficult being just a kid at home but also being responsible for my younger siblings. They didn't always appreciate being bossed about by their elder brother and consequently, sometimes things happened that shouldn't have. For instance, when we had gas lighting, during a ball playing game the gas mantle got broken. We had no idea how to put a new one on and had to sit in the dark until Mother, who had been visiting her mother two doors away, came home. Of course I, Peter, was responsible and I got a smack for allowing them to play with a ball indoors.

When we had electricity put in, it was like magic. Just by the press of a switch the light came on and with another press, it went off again. The younger ones would say, 'Can I have a go?' but the novelty soon wore off. At least I didn't have to consider their breaking the gas mantle from then on!

I remember one time when my brother Walter's classroom had got wet through because of a burst water main, or something like that. So his class got put into mine and it became a very big class for the teacher to manage. Being in my class proved to be very unfortunate for Walter and, as it turned out, particularly for me one lunchtime.

We use to play football at lunchtimes in the playground; we never went home for lunch because it was too far to go. Lunch was sandwiches: sometimes jam, sometimes dripping, and occasionally we got offered a school meal when someone was absent. We had a sponge ball to kick about with, and one time it was kicked onto the school roof and got lodged in the gutter. Brave Peter was the idiot who shinned up the drain pipe to get it. Having managed to free it and throw it (and others I found there) down to my playmates I suddenly realised how high I was and panicked a bit as to how I was to get down. I did manage to get down but by this time the teacher had come out and I was caught in the act. I got put up in front of the class – the class that now included my brother – and got six strokes of the cane on each hand. I was being sort of heroic and trying not to cry and indeed managed not to but when I looked over at my brother, he was crying his eyes out; it was a bit too much for him to witness his big brother getting the stick.

When our Walt and I were about seven or eight years old we were able to go to the pictures on a Saturday afternoon. It was called the 'tuppenny rush' because it use to cost *tuppence* and we would queue up outside until the doors opened and then *rush* in to get the best seats we could. There was a poor old man (for whom we had a nickname but I cannot recall it now) who use to try and keep some semblance of order and shout, 'Sit down and keep quiet or the pictures won't start and if there's any noise whilst they're showing then I'll kick you out.' This always seemed to work. We used to watch cartoons and cowboy and science fiction films, which were all very exciting, and then re-enact them on the way home. We watched one film about going to the moon; that of course, has now been achieved but in those days it was complete but fascinating fiction.

It was about this time too, that Mother started another moneymaking scheme: making hearth rugs. We kids had to help by cutting up the old bits of cloth Mum had scrounged from folks around the area. She would wash them and then tell us how big or how small the bits had to be. These bits were then pegged to make patterns in the hearth-sized pieces of sacking material she stretched out between the backs of two chairs, often using us kids as counterweights to keep the cloth taut. Lord knows where she got this sacking from but she did. She made quite a few rugs and sold them.

As I mentioned, I was nine years old when the war started and it didn't mean too much to me or the rest of us kids, except for the black-out, which meant that we couldn't play outside in the evenings, certainly in the winter. But there was one exciting moment when a Nazi plane that had been bombing Sheffield obviously dropped his bombs in the wrong place, as one fell in our backyard. Luckily we were in the shelter, for we went there at about six o'clock each evening during the air raids. I only remember bombing raids being at night-time although London, Birmingham and Coventry were suffering daylight raids too. The bomb in our yard blew in the doors and windows of the houses and slates off the roofs but fortunately there was not much structural damage. That night, after the 'all clear' had sounded, we were all evacuated to the town hall assembly rooms where we were given bedding and stayed all night. Although our mother was with us, Father was working a night shift and when the news of the bombing filtered through to the mines, those with homes in the bombed area were allowed to leave early. I'm sure that Dad would have been told that his wife and kids were all okay and being looked after at the town hall. However it must have been a hell of a shock for him to see the house with the doors and windows blown in. For us kids it didn't have any element of danger or fear; it was just another exciting adventure.

There were one or two other bombs that came down near us during this air raid; one of them destroyed Lovelee's, a local grocer's store, where they used to sell sweets and food and such. The building had to be demolished and our lot, with a few other enterprising mates from the area, collected up all the wooden doors and rafters and chopped them into sticks. We then took these around the neighbourhood selling them as kindling for tuppence a bucketful. This saved them having to chop up their own. We didn't make a fortune but every little helped.

Apart from this one bombing incident the war hardly touched us. We went to school and played games just as we had always done but of course those families who had grown-ups in the services would have seen it differently.

It was shortly after this that Dad came out of the mines, owing to worsening bad health. He had problems with his lungs and breathing and he got a job as a storeman in a local factory, Habershon's: a different one to the one where Mother worked.

The effect of the war was that our living standards weren't as high as they might have been had we not had a war. This was mainly due to the rationing system and lack of delicacies such as bananas and other things from overseas. Funnily enough it wasn't a case of 'what you don't have you don't miss' but rather 'what you don't have you covet most'.

We had a greyhound track about 600 yards from our house and almost weekly there would be racing. We youngsters weren't allowed in but we would sit on the wall and watch, and occasionally bet our halfpennies amongst ourselves. But mostly some adult would come and shoo us away.

One money-making scheme for us youngsters was to go around to the elderly people in the area and ask if there were any errands we could run for them: collecting groceries or suchlike. Remember that amongst most of the families there was no such thing as pocket money back then as parents were too poor for that. Occasionally you might get something if your father was lucky on the horses or dogs – perhaps a bag of sweets or suchlike and you would try to make these last for a week if you could.

We also had a scam going with empty bottles. Most liquids like beer and pop were sold in glass bottles, with the cost of the bottle factored into the price of the drink. In those days these glass bottles were collected, washed and reused. To encourage people to give the empties back you got a penny for each bottle you returned. Now we knew that the empties were kept in the yard at the back of Schofield's garage, in crates. We used, now and again, to get into the yard and 'rescue' a number of the bottles! Over the next few days we'd take them back to the shop and collect the pennies. After a while Mr Schofield got suspicious and started to mark the empties. Our scam was discovered when one of my mates got caught. He had been greedy and taken the same bottle back four times!

Christmas was always special, not only for the school holiday but for the magic of the tree, the lights and its trimmings and baubles and for the odd pennies we collected for carol singing. Christmas presents weren't many:

just a new penny or an orange and apple and sometimes our parents would produce the odd toy.

Another money-making scheme was to go first-footing on New Year's Eve. This was really marvellous because we were allowed to stay up and go out with our faces blackened, with pieces of coal and wood, to visit our neighbours just before midnight, shouting:

Old year out new year in
please can you spare a new year's gift.
If you haven't got a penny a ha'penny will do.
If you haven't got a ha'penny, then God bless you,'

and then knock at the door. Then they would ask you in and probably give you a jam tart or mince pie or something and a penny if you were lucky. One time we were really lucky and got sixpence, which was absolutely fantastic. We ran all the way home with that, not feeling it was necessary to visit any more neighbours.

Mother had credit at Schofield's store and would get a bill once a week that she would check very carefully before paying any of it off. We kids had permission to go and get things if we needed them whilst both our parents were out at work, but only within the constraints of the rationing system. We had to be very careful not to buy any, what mother would call, frivolous items such as chocolates or toffees. So what we used to do was nick the occasional toffee or other such sweet out of the jars whilst someone created a noise so that Mr Schofield the shopkeeper was distracted. Mr Schofield was a very nice man but we did use to take advantage of him from time to time. Brother Walter was an early entrepreneur – he would buy or sometimes steal a bag of fruit gums worth three-ha'pence, then sell them to the other kids at four for a penny!

During the long summer school holidays we were often visited by aunties and uncles on my mother's side. My mum's relatives all seemed to live close by, whilst my father's family lived on the other side of the town and we hardly ever saw them. This meant we had many cousins and I remember Auntie Gladys and Uncle Harold were frequent visitors with their two kids Leslie and Laureen. We called Leslie 'Les' and he was much the same age as my brother Jim. Laureen would usually pair off with our Mona. Jim and Les would always get up to all sorts of pranks. We had a long back yard that we used to play football in. In the bottom house lived a family called Mann and they had a hen coop, where they kept lots of

*1. Mother (left) and Auntie Gladys during one of those long school holidays*

hens. This was a good thing from our parents' point of view because all the neighbouring families could buy their eggs from them cheaper than they could in the shops. However Mr Mann was a bit of a tartar and if anybody went near his chickens he would chase them off. On one particular occasion our ball was kicked into the hen coop. Now I don't know whether it was deliberate or not but we did manage to get our cousin Les to climb up the side of the shed and onto the roof of the hen coop to get the ball back. But as he was walking across the roof of the shed it collapsed and Les went through. Holy Moses, you should have heard the noise those hens made when this happened, squawking and feathers flying everywhere. Everybody else scarpered leaving poor Les shouting, 'Get me out, get me out,' above the racket of all those chickens. Well, Mr Mann came out and oh was he furious. We all thought it was a real laugh; we were all hiding in various places in the yard where Mr Mann couldn't see us but he knew we were there. 'All you little bleeders, if I see any of you down here again, I'll take that ball and shove it up your arse.' He took our ball and we never got it back either. I don't think poor Les ever lived that down, for he got held by his ear and marched round to our house where Mr Mann

13

demanded that someone pay for the damage to his hen coop. I can't remember what the final outcome was but poor Peter was blamed, yet again, for letting Les get into trouble.

There was another episode of which I'm not particularly proud but which did seem to single me out as a leader at the time. This was to do with the Schofield's garage – remember their yard was used to store bottles. They use to keep all their spare stock in a garage which was normally bolted and padlocked. Unbeknown to the Schofields, if you pulled on the bolt a gap opened up at the top of the doors that a small person could get through. Goaded on by my friends and younger brothers I climbed over the top and dropped into the garage and handed them a big box of chocolate biscuits. Having collected the booty from me they all scarpered, leaving me in the garage. Luckily I could get out and I saw them running down the road handing out the biscuits to each other. I soon caught them up, however, and got what was left off them. As I said I'm not particularly proud of this now but that's the sort of pranks that I got up to – we never did anything more serious or devious than that.

Football was the popular sport and we had a street team. We use to play other street teams, all of which had names; ours was the 'Brickfield Tin Can Dribblers'. Others had names like the 'Wing Street Wanderers', 'Rutland Street Ragged Arsed Rovers' and the 'Ferham Road Foulers'. On Sunday mornings there was always a match of some sort played in Ferham Park. In our team we all wanted to be known as renowned pros – in my case I was always Bryn Jones, a famous Wolves and Arsenal Welsh international.

The usual lads who played in our team, as I remember, were Derek Fawkes, Derek and Albert Harper, two other brothers Geoff and Gordon Dunkerley, Eric Read (Tupman), Colin Bell, Derek Richardson, Georgie Charlesworth, 'Digger' Cope and Geoff Poole plus myself, brother Walter and later brother Harry. This is not a comprehensive list; there were others perhaps who, if and when they read this, might identify themselves.

CHAPTER 3

# After school and football

I LEFT SCHOOL WHEN I WAS fourteen and really wanted to. I was a very poor scholar, never taking much notice of what people were trying to teach me. I would go so far as to say I hated school, especially mental arithmetic – I could not catch on to what they were trying to tell me.

I went to work at Joby Lees, a small machine shop handling metal plates, grinding them down to a flat surface for sign-writing purposes. I was working with real craftsmen and got paid about seven and six a week, I think. Mum was delighted to take that off of me and in return gave me sixpence. Now sixpence in those days was very good. You could take a girl to the pictures and have enough left to buy some fish and chips on the way home.

However football was my main aim and main game – I wanted to be a professional footballer. I followed my home team Rotherham United assiduously and would go to see them play wherever they went if I could, although I would rather be playing myself. I joined a club named Rotherham Boys' Welfare Club which was in the centre of town. In the club were table tennis tables and snooker tables. You could play lotto, snakes and ladders and draughts but no card games – we weren't allowed to play card games as I remember. And there was a canteen.

Enid, the girl who sat next to me at school and used to get me into trouble, was now at the local girls' high school continuing her education and she and other girls used to help out in the canteen serving us with tea, soft drinks and buns. Enid's mum used to help out washing the football strips, so I would see Enid on a regular basis. At that time she was a part of our gang and we were just good friends. There was no question of being girl- or boyfriend; I think we were far too young. Anyway, if you went out with a girl it interfered with the amount of time you had to play football, so that was no good. And girls didn't play football anyway, so they weren't popular. Of course they were going to get very popular later on, but in my early teen years it was only football that got my attention. I was never interested in courting; my father had told me that a penny bun cost tuppence when you had a girlfriend, and if you only had a penny . . . well?

Enid didn't leave school until she was seventeen but again, that's for later.

I loved football and was rather a good player if I say so myself. I know this to be a fact because at the age of fourteen I was put up to play in the intermediate team. At that time there were three boys' leagues in the Sheffield area: a junior league for boys between fourteen and sixteen, an intermediate league for boys between sixteen and eighteen; and a senior league which was for guys of eighteen to twenty-one. The Boys' Club had a team in all of the leagues.

We played in what was called the Sheffield and Hallamshire area which included elements of Barnsley, Doncaster, Sheffield and of course, Rotherham. All these teams used to play each other on Saturday afternoons. Because of my ability I progressed very rapidly from the juniors to the intermediate team and even, because of some flu bug that was flying around, a couple of games with the seniors. This was lucky for me because during those few games I was picked up by a scout called Mr Etherington, who had once been a pre-war Wolverhampton Wanderers player and who was now scouting for Wolves in the South Yorkshire area. Indeed Wolverhampton Wanderers had a nursery team called Wath Wanderers for which team Mr Etherington used to find players, Wath being a village just outside Rotherham.

Wath Wanderers played at a slightly higher level and mainly in the Barnsley area but this did extend further out into other little villages and places near us. Mr Etherington took me down for a trial at Wolverhampton by train via Birmingham – this was the first time I had been out of South Yorkshire. The trial was quite rigorous as I remember. It wasn't just about playing football; you had to jump over benches and suchlike, so I think they were testing your fitness as well as your ability. The trials extended over two days and we stayed overnight in the house of a woman that Mr Etherington knew. Anyway I was taken on by Wolverhampton but as I was only fifteen, wasn't able to sign for them or get paid except for expenses.

We had a family bust-up about this time, and we were all split up, but more about that later.

Eventually Mr Etherington came back to my house to discuss the matter with my Auntie Nellie and Uncle Bill with whom I was now living. Wolverhampton Wanderers wanted me to go and live in the Wolverhampton area, in a boarding house which was run by a woman on their behalf. This was where all the juniors lived and she brought them up like a kind of auntie. My Auntie Nellie was dead against it and I thought at the time it was because she loved me so much she didn't want me to leave. However I found out in later years that it was because she didn't want to lose my wages as it was an important part of the household income.

Anyway I did go down to Wolverhampton for the odd game and did on these occasions make a bit of money out of the expenses I was paid. This was because it didn't actually cost me anything, for they would send me a prepaid return rail ticket and then pick me up from the station, taking me back to the station after the match. I was also continuing to play for the Boys' Club and did, on a couple of occasions, 'guest' for Whinney Hill St Peter's against an Italian POW camp team. Whilst I didn't play for Wath, occasionally I would go to Wath to keep up my training, usually on Tuesday and Thursday evenings, when a few of us would get together and kick a ball about. I was set to become a professional footballer. Unfortunately, at the age of seventeen, I was playing for the Boys' Club against Whinney Hill St Peter's when I broke my leg in a tackle with Roy Fairhurst. Roy's parents were customers of the opticians where Enid worked – there she was again. However the accident left my leg in plaster and proved to be the end of my dreams of becoming a professional footballer.

Around this time Enid had her eighteenth birthday party and I was invited to go. All of her high school girlfriends together with most of the footballers were there and some of those things that the girls wrote on my plaster you wouldn't believe. There they were, all from good families, even toffs perhaps, and you wouldn't have thought they knew such things but what they wrote was shocking. Things like 'Did I leave my knickers in your house?' or 'How was it the first time?', 'Can you still do it with your plaster on?' and things like that which was very risqué for those days. Luckily only I knew these comments were there, and those people I chose to show them to from time to time. I had no idea then that Enid, in the future, was to become my wife.

When it came to have the plaster removed by a male nurse I sat in a chair waiting for him to saw it off. I sat there in this room and waited and waited for him to get cracking. Eventually I said to him, 'Are you ever going to take this "pot" off?' He replied, 'No, not yet, I haven't finished reading it all!'

During this period I changed my job twice. I left my first job at Joby Lees and went to work at Turton and Platts in Wincobank, on the border between Rotherham and Sheffield. But the long travel and shift work was a bit much so I left and went to work at Moreton's Wagon Works nearer to home. They made railway wagons and initially I was the blacksmith's striker. However I was too slight of build to give the smith the power he needed, so they made me the storekeeper's assistant – a real cushy job!

I was due to join the army for National Service at eighteen. Because I was much younger than the rest of my footballing mates they kept disappearing as they were called up for their National Service. This meant that I knew what regiments they were going to and so, when it came to my turn, I asked to go into the King's Own Yorkshire Light Infantry where most of my mates had gone. I never actually got into that regiment, however, although I did bump into them from time to time.

Prior to breaking my leg I had never wanted to go into the army because it would delay me from achieving my goal of becoming a professional footballer. Now things were different.

CHAPTER 4

# Family break–up

A BOUT A YEAR AFTER THE WAR ENDED, a distressing period of time ensued. Mother, whether she met him through work or socially, it's not clear, was rumoured to have started an affair with Joe Whelan, a local bachelor. Father had inklings of what was being surmised but had absolutely no proof. However, he, Dad, started to drink heavily. Now almost always when he went out he would come back drunk and accuse Mother of having been unfaithful and sometimes hit her. It was becoming intolerable in our house. We kids were becoming distraught and dreading Father coming home. We would all be put to bed, or latterly, not me or Walter; we would go up after the younger ones. But once the ruckus started the younger ones would get up again and be sat on the stairs crying. Walter or I would try to explain and console them but it was an awful time which lasted for about eighteen months. Things finally came to a head when Father, stoned (drunk) out of his mind, went too far and beat Mother

*2. My father (bottom left) with his mates – one of the few photos we have of him*

*3. Dad with Ian (2½) outside Wentworth Sanatorium 1959*

up. Mona, Walter and I, in fact all the lot of us, were involved. The younger ones in night clothes were trying to stop the row but unfortunately the injuries to Mum were quite severe. Mona went next door to ask Mrs Dobson to come and get my mother, which she did. And that started the break-up of what used to be a happy family.

It was agreed that Mum would not live with Dad again, so she went to live with one sister, then another and finally settled with her mother, my grandmother, taking our sister Mona with her. We boys stayed with Dad but without Mum's efforts it was hopeless. The state of the house became horrible and almost untenable – something had to be done. It was: we boys were farmed out to Auntie Nellie (my mother's sister) and lived with her, in my case only until I was eighteen, when I went into the army. After this point I never lived permanently with any of my family ever again.

Mother did eventually move into a council house in Thorpe Hesley and reeled in her kids, where they settled down nicely. Grandma had died in the meantime and so Granddad (her father) moved in with her.

Dad's sickness was getting worse – the same symptoms that had caused him to leave mining – and was more in evidence. He was eventually given a bed-sit in a new housing estate but not long afterwards he was admitted to a sanatorium in Wentworth and later died at the age of sixty-one. Dad was buried in St Bede's churchyard in the same grave as his mother – my grandmother. Before his death, we had corresponded and during his time in the sanatorium, when I had a UK posting, I was able to visit him from time to time. Indeed he was able to see and hold his first grandson – my eldest, Ian – before he died, for by this time I had married Enid. But now, I'm getting ahead of myself.

In between all this Mother and my siblings settled down and Mother eventually married Joe Whelan.

# Chapter 5

# National Service to Regular
# (1948–49)

WITH MY PLASTER OFF I thought that I might not be accepted for National Service as my leg was rather withered. But no chance – I think that they would have taken anybody who could breathe at that time. So I was passed as A1 and went in on 15 April 1948 and was ordered to report to a place called Bordon in Hampshire. I immediately found life there for me was very good. I loved it; I now had a bed to myself and three full meals a day – heaven! I seemed to be liked by everyone and got on with people – well, most of the time. But I hadn't known then that I was starting a career that would last for 43 years and 278 days and take me through the ranks and throughout the world.

*4. Raw recruit*

On my arrival there was an incident with a letter I had from Wolverhampton Wanderers. This was supposedly meant to have asked for permission for me to be released from time to time to play with the Wolverhampton juniors' team. This involved the Corporal on duty, who was introducing us to drill and showing us what to do when we got to our barracks: what bed we could have and so on. Well, he asked us if we had any questions so I said, 'I've got this letter, mate,' and he screamed at me, 'Mate! I'm no mate of yours. When you address me you address me as Corporal, you little worm.' Well, I'd never been spoken to like that before but carried on nonetheless, saying, 'I've got this letter here. It's from Wolverhampton Wanderers and it's for the Commanding Officer.' He barked back, 'Commanding Officer, you? You're nobody, you'll never see the Commanding Officer, he wouldn't look at you twice,' and with that he took that bloody letter and tore it in half. It wasn't the best introduction to the army.

But it didn't put me off. I loved the army. I was really proud, I did things that I wanted to and I did them with quickly learned skill and was really enthusiastic. I was good in the gym and good in the drill square. I didn't know I could shoot but learnt very quickly and turned out to be a good shot. I was a fast learner (and subsequently found out that I was a good teacher too) and after a week's basic training I was put on to a thing called X cadre which was for recruits that looked as if they might make potential officers, or potential non-commissioned officers (NCOs). This was the result of having good marks in the 'matrix' test which we took under supervision of the Royal Army Education Corps (RAEC) Sergeants on our second day in the army. Being on X cadre didn't give us any special privileges. We did everything the other recruits did like drill, shooting and the physical training (PT) exercises and lived in the same barrack rooms and everything else, except that we did extra lessons. These were things like map reading that the normal recruit didn't do. We did these lessons in the evenings and at the weekend which was a bit of a bore sometimes because these were the only times you could have any time to yourself.

On Sunday mornings there was always a church parade. When I went into the army I was told to tell them I was a Catholic, an RC. I said, 'OK, why?' and was told that if I told them I was an RC I wouldn't have to go on church parade on Sundays. So my documents recorded this. The very first Sunday they said, 'RCs fall out,' and we all stood to one side whilst the others marched to church. However the person who told me to tell them I was an RC must have been a right joker because those of us left behind had to do all the clearing up in the barrack rooms, the toilets and everything else. The old Father, the Roman Catholic priest, use to come round and say, 'Gather together,' and we'd gather round and talk about this, that and the other but generally speaking we never got any privileges whatsoever for being Catholics. So after a while I said I don't want to be a Catholic any more, I'd rather go to church. But no way, once it was down on paper that was it.

I must have shown some promise in X cadre because at the end of our training I was given a lance corporal's stripe together with a few others from the cadre. So technically, I suppose, I was never ever a private soldier. I came straight from being a recruit to a lance corporal. Many of the people in my intake were Yorkshire people and like me had come down from Yorkshire to Hampshire to train. There were other people there from Geordies to Brummies and Welsh kids and Scots, a real conglomerate really. However our intake had been earmarked for the King's Own Yorkshire Light Infantry (KOYLI) so they supposedly wanted a Yorkshire lad in charge and chose me. They gave me this stripe and I was all set to join the KOYLI. But no, lo and behold they made me the draft conducting NCO and sent me with sixty-one men to reinforce the Oxf. & Bucks. Light Infantry (LI) in Germany. I wasn't supposed to have been in charge of these men; a full corporal was meant to be the leader and I was supposed to be his assistant. However the day before we were due to leave he went sick and so they left it to me to take the men, and the paperwork and everything and get them there; which I duly did.

Fortunately when we got to the Oxf. & Bucks. LI in Lüneburg, Germany (where incidentally, the World War II peace treaty was signed) the battalion was short of junior NCOs, so I kept my stripe and was posted to D company.

My first Company Commander (OC) was Major (Pat) Montgomery and my Platoon Commander and Platoon Sergeant were 2nd Lieutenant (Bill) Chevis and Sergeant Derek Hornblower. Other junior NCOs with me were Harry Jones and Tommy Hunter, who had come to the battalion from the KOYLI, and shortly after I arrived, these two were promoted to full Corporals. Joe Hayden and Doc Kempster had come through the same route as me and had also kept their stripes. One of the private soldiers was Graham (Punchy) Morris who became a good mate of mine, as we were both in the boxing team. I mention all these names now, for they will appear often in later chapters.

*5. Religious retreat, Bielefelt. Peter front*
*row 2nd from left*

*6. Signatures on reverse of photo*

Immediately on joining the regiment I went on a junior leader's course. This was run by the 2nd Battalion Grenadier Guards in Sennelager, another place in Germany. My Platoon Sergeant there was a Grenadier called Tom Taylor, yet another bloke I would come into contact with over the years.

During my stay in Lüneburg, the fact that I was a Catholic came in handy. I was sent to a place called Bielefelt to have a week's religious retreat. It was like a holiday camp.

Also, for a short time whilst serving in Lüneburg, I was involved in the last stages of operation 'Woodpecker' in which most of the forests in Germany were being cut down to provide the UK with timber – presumably as reparation – to help repair our bomb-damaged buildings. The irony of this was that we were in barrack rooms with wood-burning stoves but were often without any wood and consequently went to bed freezing. We were working with an abundance of timber all day, yet couldn't have any of it for our own use – how galling!

I remained a lance corporal for almost twelve months before I got paid for it, by which time we had left Lüneburg and gone to Göttingen, still in Germany.

From our camp in Göttingen we use to do patrols along the new line that had been drawn by the Russians to separate East from West Germany as a result of the Potsdam Agreement. We were on the border with all the barbed wire entanglements. This was known as the 'Iron Curtain'.

During our time there, a nasty incident took place. A Corporal of our regiment had been out shooting rabbits and had strayed into East Germany by accident where he was apprehended by the Russians. Our whole battalion was put on high alert and our platoon was ordered to go and get

The **Iron Curtain**, a term coined by Winston Churchill in 1946, symbolised the ideological and physical boundary dividing Europe into two separate areas from the end of WWII in 1945 until the end of the Cold War in 1991.

The United Kingdom, France, Japan, Canada, the United States and many other countries had backed the White Russians against the Bolsheviks during the 1918–1920 Russian Civil War, and the Soviets had not forgotten the fact.

Churchill feared that the United States might return to its pre-war isolationism, leaving the exhausted European states unable to resist Soviet demands.

The Iron Curtain took the shape of border defences between the countries of Western and Eastern Europe, most notably the Berlin Wall, which served as a longtime symbol of the Curtain as a whole.

During the time that I was on border duties in Göttingen Stalin, the Soviet leader, was blockading Berlin, which he believed would result in a united Germany under communist control. In response, the Western Allies organised the Berlin Airlift to carry supplies to the people of Berlin, a massive and highly successful operation that lasted almost a year and humiliated the Soviets who had repeatedly claimed it could never work. This humiliation no doubt fuelled the strained relations on the border between East and West.

him back. Unfortunately during this operation one of our party, a Private Knill, was shot and tragically later died, or so I was led to believe.

This incident was mentioned in the *Regimental Chronicles* of 1948 although the narrative fails to mention that Private Knill died from his chest wound. Some extracts follow.

We did border patrols for a while before we got word that we were being posted to Salonika in Northern Greece which sounded very exciting and exotic to me and I was keen to go. Anyway they said that anyone who had less than a year to serve couldn't go unless they signed on. So I immediately signed on for what I believed was 'five and seven': five years regular service and seven years reserve service.

CHRONICLE.
1948

## INCIDENT ON BORDER OF ANGLO-SOVIET ZONES

A NUMBER of very inaccurate reports have appeared in the press about an incident which occurred just before Christmas on the boundary between the British and Russian zones near the ancient city of Duderstadt. The following is the real story and by way of comparison the Tass Agency report of the same incident is also given.

On the afternoon of December 15th, 1948, three non-commissioned officers of the Regiment went out shooting in a party organized by an Intelligence Officer of the Control Commission. The shoot was in the vicinity of Immingerode near Duderstadt and very close to the border between the British and Russian zones. The officer omitted to explain to the non-commissioned officers that they were close to the border nor did he point out where it lay. During the course of the afternoon one of the non-commissioned officers wounded a hare. He ran after the animal and fired several more shots at it and whilst so doing crossed over into the Russian Zone.

A Russian patrol appeared on the scene and fired one or two bursts of machine-rifle fire over his head. He perforce had to accompany the patrol back to their headquarters. The remainder of the party returned and reported what had happened.

Explanation by the author:

Platoon of 'D' Company (my Platoon) was dispatched to the area. Two sections went to ground lining the road and the other section escorted the Adjutant's party to the Russian sentry post.

The Adjutant, with the two policemen and the interpreter, went ahead and the section marched some fifty yards in rear. This officer and the policemen were entirely unarmed and the section carried rifles but no ammunition, since the visit was purely to make a formal request for the non-commissioned officer to be returned. All this was strictly in accordance with orders laid down by higher authority.

On arrival at the Russian sentry post at about 2100 hrs two Russian sentries appeared and the Adjutant made his request, via the interpreter and the Russian-speaking German policeman. After a minute or two of talk the Russian sentries began to get very excited and fired some bursts of machine rifle-fire into the air, whereupon some four or five more Russian soldiers turned out of the guardroom and proceeded to fire bursts of machine rifle-fire into the air over the heads and in between the ranks of the British section. Whilst this *feu-de-joie* was going on Private Knill was shot in the chest. There is no doubt that this was done accidentally as the Russian soldiers were all in a state of high excitement. In order to avoid further trouble the Adjutant ordered the section to make no resistance and to accompany the Russian soldiers, whilst he himself succeeded in dragging Private Knill back into safety.

CHAPTER 6

# Regular: Greece, Cyprus and Egypt
# – PYTHON
# (1949–52)

WE WERE IN GREECE TO PATROL the Greek/Bulgarian border to help stop infiltration of communists and to take advantage of the many training areas that were there. One place in particular was Khortiatis Camp in the hills above our main headquarters – Sobraon Barracks – which companies occupied in turns, a month at a time. We did this for nearly a year, and other than training and the odd sports event, I can't recall anything of real significance happening, except that on Christmas Day we were served our Christmas dinner by the officers and sergeants – it was nice not to have to queue up. Then in January 1950 the whole battalion moved to Cyprus: Waynes Keep Camp in Nicosia.

By this time I was doing well on the sporting field. Amongst other sports I was in the boxing team. We had a Sergeant PT Instructor, Sgt. Powell of the Army Physical Training Corps (ATPC). He was really hard and used to put us through it. We had to get up at half past five (Reveille was always six o'clock in the morning) and report to the guard room in our tracksuits or clothes similar to what you would call tracksuits today: trousers, shirts and towels, and we always had to take along our boxing gloves. When you did road walks and runs you had to keep punching and not let your hands drop below your waist. I'm sure this stood us in good stead when we were in the ring, where you had to keep your hands up anyway to stop yourself from being hit! It was good training.

Our road runs would include skipping and hopping and running backwards and all sorts of things to get you fit. We'd also do an hour of gym work: shadow boxing, punch bags, skipping, balance-walking and sparring, and then we'd go back for breakfast. And we used to have steaks. Steaks for breakfast! It was excellent. Another great thing about this is that we never had to do any regimental duties, no night guards or working parties – we got well and truly looked after.

*7. Limbering up for the Cyprus boxing events*

By now I'd was becoming popular and known and I'd also been elevated to full corporal after attending a junior NCOs' course. 'Punchy' Morris was made a lance corporal after this course and became a PT Instructor.

And then of course there was the football. I was always going to be selected. I was probably one of the first names on the sheet, being a pretty good player and more or less known as one of the better players in the regimental team. So there was a certain element of being left off regimental duties because of that too. It seems to me, and I swear to this day, that all my sporting and athletic ability came in useful for helping me get promotion. Not exactly favouritism but nevertheless giving me an edge.

The first time this happened was when I was one of five corporals up for one place as sergeant. The hierarchy had decreed that our battalion's role had changed and we were to become a stronger fighting force. We were to be given more heavy weapons, such as medium machine guns (MMGs), anti-tank weapons and heavier calibre mortars, together with an assault pioneer platoon. Thus the MMG platoon, mortar platoon, anti-tank platoon and assault pioneer platoon became Support (S) Company, made up mainly by personnel from D Company; now disbanded.

Unfortunately we didn't have any instructors or anybody who knew anything about the Vickers MMG, so all the MMG NCOs had to go back to England to be taught how to instruct on using them. The point I was trying to make earlier about these five corporals is that we were trying to find a sergeant to fit into the new MMG Platoon for whom there was now a vacancy. For some reason we needed two sergeants: a gunnery sergeant and a normal admin. sergeant – that is how it was at that time but it is probably different today.

For the uninitiated: you normally had four rifle companies and a headquarters (administration) company. Each rifle company had three platoons and a company HQ. In HQ Company there was a signals platoon, mechanical transport (MT) platoon, quartermaster's (QMs) section, band and bugles, intelligence section, public relations (PR) and regimental police. Regimental HQ is made up of orderly room and admin. staff, pay office and post room, Commanding Officer (CO), second in command (2IC) and adjutant. As the MMG platoon was forming up they needed more NCOs than you would normally get in a platoon, so the regiment needed another sergeant. These five corporals were all possibilities and eligible for promotion but I was the only one the CO knew. You couldn't expect a man who has six or seven hundred men under his command to know every one of them. Naturally he would get recommendations from the individual's superior officer but he wouldn't know them personally. But he knew me because the day before he'd been watching a football match where he'd seen me score the winning goal against the RAF team. 'Ah, Corporal Lawless, that was a good goal you scored yesterday,' he said to me. And it just showed what the army was like in those days because I got the sergeant's vacancy – but not yet. So I'm sure, certainly in those early days, my sporting prowess gave me an advantage over the other poor sods who might well have been better soldiers than me. However I believe that I did become a good NCO and eventually a good officer.

Whilst serving in Salonika my brother Walter had been called up for National Service and because I was now a regular I was able to claim him into my regiment, which I duly did, only to find that when he arrived he was posted to 'A' Company who were stationed in Athens, 'flying the flag'. So we didn't meet up until we were in Cyprus. He was eventually made a lance corporal (LCpl) PT instructor, and – shock horror – his name was now usually the first on the football team sheet; from my last seeing him,

8. *Combined Services Team v APOEL a Cypriot professional team, me (front middle),
brother Walter on my right (we lost 2–1 but Walt scored the goal)*

he had developed into a great player. He was so good he became a regular
in the combined services team, for which I only got selected occasionally.

I remember Walt had to go to Egypt to take his three weeks PT course
so he at least got to visit one more country but all good things come to an
end; his service finished and he was demobbed. Shortly after he went home
the regiment moved to Egypt and it was there that my promotion to
sergeant took place. By now the MMG Platoon was well established and I
went home to the UK on a course to learn about the MMG platoon
sergeant's role and responsibilities. The course lasted for six weeks and at
the end of it I was given two weeks' leave which were to prove to be the
most significant fourteen days of my life.

The course finished on a Friday and I went to my mother's house where
all my family were now living. On the Saturday night I went with brother
Walter to a dance. Again I went along mostly to be with my former mates
and to have a few beers at the interval. Women weren't a mystery to me;
having grown up with a younger sister. So I managed to get a few dances.
Afterwards we went to catch our bus for home where we bumped into
Enid Paine and her mother who had been to the pictures. Whilst we waited

we got talking and Mrs Paine took me to one side and told me that Enid had just broken her engagement and was feeling a bit low. I knew nothing of this of course; I didn't even know she had been engaged. Anyway Mrs Paine invited me to tea the next day, Sunday, and I went. During my time there Mrs Paine (Gladys) — now obviously in the role of matchmaker — asked me to take Enid for a walk.

We went to the bluebell wood to pick bluebells but there were so many people there picking bluebells that we had to pick bluebells! However we did talk and during the rest of my leave we went out every night and got to know each other better. It was fairly obvious that there was an attraction between us.

By the time I was due to return to my regiment Enid promised to write to me, and she did. I replied and in one of my letters I asked her to marry me. I'd told her I wasn't leaving the army so she would have to be an army wife — she accepted.

Meanwhile I was fighting another battle in the battalion. I must explain: in existence at the time was a regulation called PYTHON which entitled anyone who had served overseas for three years to have a home posting. Before meeting up with Enid I had absolutely no intention of claiming PYTHON; why should I? I'd just been made sergeant and my career was looking good. However, now I'd become engaged to Enid and I couldn't wait to get home. But because I'd just done a course so that I could take on the role of the MMG Platoon sergeant my company commander refused to listen to me and put me in front of the CO. The CO wasn't very pleased at my decision and pointed out that a lot of money had been spent on sending me on the MMG sergeants' course. He said that I would have to relinquish my third stripe — I don't think it had been on my uniform for more than a few weeks — and that I would be posted to the regimental depot in Oxford as a training corporal. He also said I was a fool but nevertheless wished me luck in both my career and my love life.

During the two weeks leave that I met and fell in love with Enid she had introduced me to a game called korfball. This was a Dutch game that had just arrived in the UK and Enid was playing in the Rotherham and District korfball team. They use to practise in the Herringthorpe playing fields and she took me along. With my sporting prowess I became a pretty good player in a very short period of time, just a few days in fact.

I found out that there was a general interest in this korfball. It was very popular in the Sheffield area and there were teams all over the country.

*9. Enid showing her Korfball prowess*

Korfball is played indoors or outdoors on a court more or less like netball with three sections on the court; front, centre and back. If you are playing as a defender you can only advance into the middle section and the reverse if you are an attacker. The ball is similar to a football but with more grip and bounce. Teams have six men and six women and players score by throwing the ball through the other team's basket. After two goals the teams change ends, or zones to be more precise: defenders become attackers and attackers become defenders. At half-time teams swap halves.

So when I was posted back to Cowley Barracks in Oxford (our regimental depot) as a training corporal (two stripes instead of three but I didn't mind as I could see Enid regularly) I had a job where I could get leave on a pretty frequent basis. I got forty-eight hour passes, leaving Friday night and returning Sunday night or sometimes even a seventy-two hour pass, where I didn't have to be back until Monday night. I was issued with about eight rail warrants as was my due and when these ran out I had to buy my own, although I didn't mind. Sometimes if you were lucky and you knew someone with a car you could get a lift, although cars were very rare in those days.

Now when I got leave I didn't go home to Mum's. I stayed with Enid's parents and shared a bed with Enid's brother Brian. No hanky-panky in those days!

All the korfball games were played on a Sunday so I was able to play in them and thoroughly enjoyed it. To be honest there weren't that many players in the Rotherham area of the South Yorkshire group so I managed to play in most games.

Now this is how I nearly became an international player. I was selected into the England squad from players all over the country: from up in the North – Leeds, Sheffield, Bolton and Burnley in Lancashire, as they had players there and a small local league; and certainly in South London where there was quite a big interest in korfball. The Dutch side were to play two games against area teams and an international match against England.

Anyway the international match that I remember was being played in Mitcham in Surrey. We all met there and the tournament was over three days. On the first night we arrived, the London people had arranged for us all to go in a group to Wembley Stadium where we saw the famous Harlem Globetrotters basketball team – they were over here doing displays, exhibitions and challenge matches and so on. The first day we warmed up, the second was for all the knockout stages and the last day was the finals of the area tournament – Rotherham got to the semi-finals. The match England v Holland was to be the finale. I was picked in the squad but was only a reserve and never played. One of our Rotherham players, Arthur Gelsthorpe, played through the whole game – we lost 7–2. The London people found us accommodation with other players. Enid and I and another couple stayed with a family in Clapham. They were very nice people and we did stay in touch with them for a while but with all the travelling that I did around the world with the army we eventually lost touch.

PART 2

# Married Life in the Army

CHAPTER 7

# Corporal,
# Cowley Barracks, Oxfordshire
# (1952)

ENID AND I GOT MARRIED on Thursday 1 January 1953 at Dalton Parish
Church in Rotherham. In those days New Year's Day wasn't a public
holiday but the shops did have half-day closing on Thursdays, so that's why
we chose this date, so all our friends and family could come to the wedding
which was at 3 o'clock. Quite a few people came to the wedding and even
more people came to the Eastwood Hotel for the reception. We had a
special room upstairs which they used for parties and suchlike – it was
pretty good if I say so myself. My brother Walter was my best man.

I got a telegram from the company commander on behalf of the other
officers at the depot, which I was very surprised about because I was only

*10. Dalton Parish Church*

*11. The bride and groom*

a corporal. I also got one from the sergeant major of the depot on behalf of all the other ranks plus one from my good mate Graham (Punchy) Morris. Graham was now also a full corporal at the depot and I asked him to come up for the wedding, so he came to Rotherham and stayed with my mother and the rest of the boys and myself for the stag night.

At my stag night we didn't get up to any funny tricks: oh no, not at all. We went to a pub for a few drinks. I had all sorts of things pinned on to my back which I didn't know about. One particular one said, 'Another one to the slaughter.' I had no idea it was there until we left at about half past ten when the pub shut and we had to pack it in.

On my previous visit to Rotherham, Enid and I had selected and bought my wedding suit at Burton's, which I left at my mother's. When I got back to Mum's house I found that my suit was in for cleaning. Apparently my brother Jim – always a favourite with Mum – had been wearing it! Fortunately we got it back next morning in time for the wedding. Jim wasn't very popular with me after that – or for a while anyway.

Walter, as best man, was supposed to control all the speakers at the reception. However Punchy Morris stood up unannounced and said:

'You'll be pleased to know that we have just received a weather forecast for the honeymoon. It goes like this: "It will be warm and close tonight with maybe a little 'son' to follow."'

Well, the room split with laughter. I don't know where he got that from but it was very funny.

So Enid and I were married. We spent our first night in Enid's bedroom in her mother's house. Gladys and Bill, her mother and father, were lovely people. They had taken to me and we got on very well together. Bill and I used to go out drinking to his local club now and again when I came up on leave, particularly if I was staying for a long weekend and was there on a Sunday night, which I usually was.

After our wedding night we went back to Oxford for a week's honeymoon. We were not sure about food and what else we might need for our first few days in Oxford so Enid's mother packed a few things in a carrier bag for us to take but Enid said, 'I'm not carrying a shopping bag when we're going out in public.' She got all huffy about it so I said, 'Mother [because I called her Mother too], give it to me. I'll carry it because I don't care.' I was in civvies clothes anyway. In this carrier bag she had put some sandwiches for the journey, a jar of beetroot, would you believe, and a tin of cocoa and a few other bits and pieces that weren't going to last us very long.

As there weren't any married quarters available the army had found us a hiring. By this time I had spent almost all my money. Remember I only had one lot of sergeant's pay because I came home on PYTHON and was reduced back to corporal. I had never saved any of my sergeant's pay and anything I'd managed to save as a corporal I spent on the wedding. Even the 7 shillings a week I'd been sending home to my mother, which was mandatory, had gone on the wedding. This had covered all the brides-maid's presents, wedding invitations, flowers and buttonholes for the wedding party. And there were the unexpected expenses . . .

Enid's father, Bill wasn't a very well off man, because being riddled with arthritis he was often out of work but he'd promised to buy a barrel of beer for the wedding. However half-way through the evening it ran out so I had to buy another. This had really cleared me out – I had about £10 to £12 to my name which wasn't very much at all if you consider that although I was going to be living in digs (the army paid the rent) I would have to pay the household bills: gas, electricity, coal and suchlike. I was going to get a marriage allowance, almost double the rate of pay, plus some other extras because I now had two mouths to feed; so that would give us about £5 a week. However I hadn't received any of this increase yet.

We got back to Oxford to Minnie and Jack, the people who owned our digs. Fortunately they were Yorkshire people; they'd both come to Oxford from Leeds many years ago so we talked the same language. However when we arrived Minnie said, 'I'm sorry to put it on you so quickly but I ordered a load of coal before you arrived and of course I expect you to pay half of it.' Well we said OK without realising that the bill for our share was £7 10s. which took away over half of the money we had left. Looking back we had to laugh because coming from being a miner's son where coal wasn't ever a problem, now I was spending my hard earned money on coal. Normally this would have been paid for by the army but because we were in digs we had to pay it ourselves. So for the rest of that week, our honeymoon week, we lived on beetroot sandwiches and cocoa.

Although we'd had no money for most of that week I'd managed to get up to the barracks and talk the paymaster into letting me have an advance on my first week's pay as a married man. Minnie offered to take Enid shopping to show her around and she told her to bring her ration book, as we still had them then, and took her to the Co-op. As Enid was about to look around the shop Minnie took hold of her arm and said, 'Once you've got whatever you want you go to that man over there to pay.'

Enid said, 'Oh, all right, but what for?'

Minnie replied, 'Never you mind, just make sure you go to *him*.'

Well, she did and afterwards Minnie pointed out that the man always marked the ration book in pencil so it was possible to rub it out and go to another cashier and get two lots of rations. Enid said, 'You can't do that, can you?' but Minnie told her she'd been getting away with this for a long time.

Well, when I came home and Enid told me about this I said, 'Bloody hell, we'll get thrown in jail for that. You need to be careful about that in future.' Enid said that Minnie seemed to have gotten away with it and when she had gone up to the man he had just winked at her so he had to be in on it too. Well, this continued for some time and I turned a blind eye as we always seemed to have plenty of food, with bacon and meat at weekends too.

After having been in Oxford for about three weeks Enid said that her Mum and Dad wanted to come down and visit. Now this coincided with Minnie and Jack going on their annual fortnight's holiday and they said that

Enid's parents could sleep in their room, so this worked out very well. The first night we were there we went out to a local pub for a meal and Enid said, 'I'll do dinner for you tomorrow night.'

I got back after work at about ten to seven and Enid produced these marvellous lamb chops (one each); nobody said anything but as she started to serve up Gladys said, 'How can you manage to get all this meat on your rations?'

So Enid told her mother about the man and his pencil and her mother went barmy, saying, 'You can't do that, it's a criminal act.'

However Bill took a different approach saying, 'Well, I don't bloody care; this is marvellous. I'm going to eat it before you tell the police.' When her parents went home Enid stopped the 'rubbing out' business.

Whilst Enid's parents were staying with us we took them on a few coach trips. We went down to Cheddar Gorge and the Wookey Hole caves in Somerset. We went up to London to the theatre one evening and saw Norman Wisdom in a play. We also visited the local pub, the Swan, a few times.

My work at the barracks had more or less settled into a day job so that I could get home most evenings. There was of course the occasional night duty as guard commander or orderly NCO, which kept me in camp.

I found my work at Cowley most exhilarating, because to train young men straight from Civvy Street and turn them into soldiers required a great deal of dedication and experience. The way the system was set up, a great deal of competitive spirit was needed. Platoon was set against platoon; in fact a shield was awarded at the end of training for the best platoon. Tests included barrack room tidiness, weapon handling and shooting, PT exercises, foot drill and personal turn-out. All these various competitions were awarded marks out of ten.

The competition was not just for the recruits, although it was all meant to be. As Corporal Instructor in charge of a section of ten men I wanted my ten to be the best platoon. But then, so did the other two corporals. For instance, I beat the other NCOs on the kit inspection test which consists of having the whole of the recruit's kit laid out neatly and smartly on his bed, and then examined by the company commander. I'm afraid I cheated. Personal kit and clothing are the responsibility of the individual but for my ten lads I took charge of their 'housewife', which is the army name for a sewing set: needles, pins, cotton, buttons, all within a cloth packet, plus the holdall, a larger cloth packet containing toothbrush,

*12. 1952 Intake at Cowley Barracks – my one and only complete intake – (me front row 3rd in from the left), Maj David Wood (front and centre), Derek Hornblower, Graham (Punchy) Morris and Doc Kempster (front row 6th, 5th and 4th in from right respectively)*

toothpaste, knife, fork and spoon, soapbox etc. I took them all home the night before the test for Enid to wash and bleach and iron, plus helping with the shine on the boots for a couple of the boys, who couldn't quite get it right. Then at 6:30 the next morning I was in the barrack room helping with the displaying of the kit on the beds. These were already laid out as I had advised them to do this the evening before and sleep on the floor, thus blankets were all folded neatly and pillows fluffed up. I supervised the final touches – and we won. Such was the keenness of the instructors who were eager to make their recruits the best!

It can't have been more than three months at the outside after my marriage when I got called into the company commander's office. Now this guy was Major David Wood MBE[3] a smashing fella. He later became a colonel and we became good friends and corresponded from time to time.

---

[3]Maj. D. Wood MBE had been a lieutenant in one of the platoons of the 52nd Oxf. & Bucks. Light Infantry that landed by glider in Normandy 24 hours prior to the main D-Day landings to take control of two strategic bridges: the Pegasus bridge over the Caen Canal and the Horsa Bridge over the river Dives. David ended his military career as a full colonel. Sadly David died whilst I was writing this book.

'I've got some news for you, Lawless' – they'd always call you by your last name, hardly ever by rank. I thought this was rather demeaning and never did this myself when I became an officer.

'Only good, I hope, sir,' I said, being cheeky.

He replied, 'It is, actually. You're going to get your third stripe back. You're going up to Strensall where you're going to be running a cadre for junior NCOs to teach them how to become instructors.'

I had only been at the Oxford depot for nine months and seen one intake come through their training and pass out, when this happened. And this after being told that I was ruining my career by refusing the MMG Sergeant's post in Egypt. So I had the best of both worlds: a beautiful woman on my arm and a promotion too.

I had first to go down to Hythe to the small arms school. Now this was Thursday and I was to start on the following Monday so I had a few days to get my kit together. The course was for six weeks. Again we didn't get all weekends free; in fact there were only two weekends when I got leave and came back up to Oxford to see Enid. Being newly married I was always keen to get back and my mates use to pull my leg by saying, 'And what's the second thing you're going to do when you get home, Peter?'

*13. Weapons Instructors' Course (me, top row, far right) Small Arms School, Hyde, Kent 1952*

I graduated from the course with an A which was the top grading. From there I went back to the depot in Cowley to pack up all my kit and equipment and my boxes at home and get transported with Enid up to Strensall in Yorkshire.

# CHAPTER 8

# Sergeant, Strensall, Yorkshire (1953–57)

I T'S FUNNY HOW THINGS work out.

Strensall was the Light Infantry Brigade HQ but it was also the King's Own Yorkshire Light Infantry (KOYLI) depot, would you believe. After joining the army to join this regiment here I was at long last, not serving in the regiment but serving in the school that was run by them.

We moved into a married quarter immediately.

Whilst I was there Enid got pregnant and we were both happy about that. I went with her to all the pre-natal clinics and in due time she went into hospital in York to give birth. Sadly the baby died at birth, which was

*14. Outside our married quarter, Strensall*

absolutely devastating for both of us. We had a name for the baby, Wendy, and it was a girl. As you might imagine carrying a baby to full-term and for Enid to live through it growing and kicking inside her for nine months only to lose it at birth was a terrible ordeal. I feared for her as she went into some sort of withdrawal and didn't want to speak about it or anything. However this didn't last for too long, about a month or so, and then she was back to her normal self again but I was really frightened at the time.

Looking back, perhaps getting myself established at Strensall was a helpful distraction from our ordeal at home. I was getting on well with everyone and had made my mark in the teaching world. I had three corporals under me and each one had a section of junior NCOs under him that he taught. I was the senior lecturer and thankfully things were going smoothly.

Toward the end of Enid's pregnancy we had a tramps' ball in the sergeants' mess and for this you dressed down. You had to look as much like a tramp as you could, women as well as men. The idea was to make the mess look as scruffy as possible with camouflage netting on the ceiling and beer barrels spread around to sit on and sawdust all over. What they had done looked really impressive. We had a best tramp's competition and the RSM (Regimental Sergeant Major) and his wife judged the best (or worse) dressed tramps. I have to say that neither Enid nor I were in contention. The beer flowed and toward the end of the evening, aided by alcohol, I asked the PMC (President of the Mess Committee) if I could do a turn for the ladies. Well, I had done this a number of times in the past and it went something like this:

This ol' coat of mine, well the outside of it's fine,
but the inside has seen some dirty weather.
So in case I get no more, this ol' coat I'll put in store.
It'll come in handy for the winter . . .

and then I took the coat off and threw it on the floor. Then of course I did the same thing with the shirt, trousers, shoes and socks. So now I was stood there in my underpants and could hear Enid saying to the women, 'Don't worry, Peter will have some swimming trunks on under there.' But little did she know that I hadn't realised that I was going to do this and so had not prepared accordingly! So I took off my underpants and turned to one side and stretched out my arms, naked as the day I was born and then covered myself up again and started to get dressed. There were gasps and ohs and arrs from the floor. I don't know what they were looking for and they probably never saw it anyway.

Well, Enid absolutely castigated me afterwards. She was really annoyed. 'You've let us down,' she said, 'you've let yourself down. What are all those women going to think? Anyway you'd better do something about it.'

So on Monday morning Peter, brave as a hero, knocked on RSM Tanner's door – of course this guy is a God among men. I went in and apologised but he said, 'Oh you're all right; it's my wife you need to apologise to.' I asked if there were any extra duties to be done – that was the way the RSM usually punished you – but he said no. I asked him if his wife was at home and went round to see her. I knocked at the door.

'Excuse me, Mrs Tanner, I've come to apologise for my behaviour on Saturday night.'

She replied, 'Oh, we're not going to worry about a little thing like that.'

Well, what she meant by that I don't know but we both burst into laughter and so did Enid when I told her.

As I mentioned, Strensall was the depot not only of the King's Own Yorkshire Light Infantry (KOYLI) but also HQ of the whole of the Light Division, that is to say all the other six Light Infantry regiments: Durham, King's Own Shropshire's, King's Own Yorkshire's, Somerset, Duke of Cornwall's and of course the Oxf. & Bucks. I was on the strength of HQ Light Division because I was teaching HQ Light Infantry courses. The courses were for junior NCOs of the different battalions to be trained how to be instructors. I taught the courses together with the warrant officer from the Small Arms School Corp. (SASC) who was of course the guiding light in all these things. He used to keep me on the straight and narrow as it were and I in turn kept all the other junior instructors in line. I had a good reputation and was popular in the mess. As weapons training sergeant one of my jobs was to supervise .22 rifle shooting in the indoor range. This included a weekly session for the wives' club; some of them became quite good shots but not Enid, she never got the hang of it.

After about eighteen months my length of service in Strensall (which would have ended at the end of the second year) was extended by another eighteen months. I moved across the square to another building where I started to teach and train potential national service officers, doing their preliminary training. This was before they went off to the War Office Selection Board, or WOSB as it was usually referred to, and then on to Eaton Hall, MONS, Sandhurst or wherever to continue their officer training at that time.

It was an excellent job that, and of course it was a higher calibre job than teaching other ranks. I trained many young potential officers who when fully commissioned went on to higher things, which proved useful later in my career.

I was still playing some sport but not getting as much time off as I had before. I did have time off, and leave of course, because the young officer training course used to operate like a university with about three months heavy training and then a month off.

When I had leave, Enid and I would go back to Rotherham, which was only thirty or forty miles down the road. Indeed many weekends we would go back and stay with Enid's Mum and Dad.

During this time my brother Walter got married and I attended in uniform.

Shortly before the end of my second eighteen month session Enid got pregnant again and she was quite heavily pregnant when I got my orders to rejoin my regiment.

*15. Me, Mum, Jim, Mona, Harry and Walt with his wife Hazel, Hazel's family and on the far right Geoff (Mona's husband)*

# CHAPTER 9

# Sergeant, CQMS and back again, Cyprus (1957–59)

O N 16 JANUARY 1956 (my twenty-sixth birthday) I left England to rejoin my regiment, the Oxf. & Bucks. Light Infantry, in Osnabrück. I was posted to SP (Support) Company and took over as MMG (Medium Machine Gun) Platoon Sergeant, the position I had lost when I left Egypt. So I suppose what goes around comes around. I had been away from the battalion for just over three years.

Although there was a married quarter available, Enid was too far into her pregnancy to make this journey sensible. In view of her earlier loss we decided that she would stay at home with her Mum and Dad. Now her father, Bill, was very proud of this and said, 'If it's a boy and born in Yorkshire he will be able to play for Yorkshire at cricket,' and this did actually happen.

About a month after arriving in Osnabrück, just before my son Ian was born, a party of officers, NCOs and sergeants visited the battleground of Waterloo in Belgium, 'Waterloo' being our regiment's principle battle honour. I was one of the sergeants that went and it was extremely interesting. It was a real eye opener for me as to how military warfare was conducted in those days – the hand to hand close quarter fighting must have been absolutely terrifying.

Our son Ian was born on 24 June 1956 and I was very proud. However I was only granted four days' leave because the regiment were finalising the move to Hong Kong and I was required to participate in this. So I came home for four days to see my new son and then returned to my regiment for the move preparations and then to help them pack up. I was responsible for ensuring all the machine gun equipment got packed up correctly so it reached the right destination in fully working order. The CO decided that we could all have fourteen days' leave prior to departure and before reporting back to a temporary camp in Southern England.

I used this time to bond more with my baby son. We were seeing people because we knew we were going away and packing up everything we needed to take with us. About ten days into the fourteen days leave we all got telegrams from the regimental HQ saying that we had to report back immediately because we were not going to Hong Kong now but to Cyprus as a standby regiment because the Suez crisis had broken out. So I had to leave poor Enid and our new youngster with all the boxes to finish packing. Alas, there wasn't going to be any married quarters so everything had to go into store.

We were informed that we were being reformed and reinforced at a place called Warley Barracks in Essex, not too far away from Brentwood. We all met there and were there for about ten to fourteen days getting kitted out in what we call khaki drill or KD, made for hotter climates, and also getting fit. We did road runs wearing full kit and loads of gym work and so on.

So off I went to Cyprus. As there were no married quarters, no families could come out so Enid and our newborn son had to stay with her mother. We had been put onto a war footing ready to move across to Egypt and the Suez Canal, ready to boost up the Paras, Commandos and others that had already gone in to sort the problems out. We were going to take over the unilateral running of the Suez Canal.

It was a real crisis.

When we arrived in Cyprus we went into different camps. As we had to build most of them before we could move in, we spent some time bivouacking in tents until they were finished.

Blow me, we hadn't been there a fortnight and we were told the crisis was all over and the troops were to be withdrawn as some sort of armistice had been agreed.

However we didn't get out of Cyprus because at the same time there was a flare-up between some misinformed people called the EOKA (*Ethniki Organosis Kyprion Agoniston* – Greek for National Organisation of Cypriot Fighters) who tried to take hold of the whole island. They wanted independence from the United Kingdom and '*Enosis*' meaning union with Greece. So there we were, prepared to fight one war and now we'd got another one on our hands. This proved to be difficult because everyone was dressed the same, so we didn't know who our enemy was.

There were two main types of Cypriot, Turkish and Greek, and how could you tell who was who because it was the Greek Cypriots who were providing the terrorists but all Cypriots looked the same. We did in effect stay there for almost three years, from 1956 till 1959 when things settled

The Suez Canal was opened in 1869 and operated by the Universal Company of the Suez Maritime Canal (Suez Canal Company) an Egyptian-chartered company partially financed by the French. The canal was strategically important to the British, who secured its control in 1882.

The canal played a major strategic role in both world wars.

After the Second World War the canal took on a new strategic significance, the transportation of oil, but Anglo-Egyptian relations began to deteriorate. The major factors in worsening relations were the declaration of Israeli Independence in 1948 and the military coup by the 'Free Officers Movement' – led by Muhammad Neguib and future Egyptian President Gamal Abdul Nasser who overthrew King Forouk and established an Egyptian Republic.

The economic potential of the Middle East, with its vast oil reserves and the Suez Canal, as well as its geo-strategic importance against the background of the Cold War, prompted Britain to consolidate and strengthen its position there. However President Nasser continued to frustrate British plans. The British expectation that the US would help tame Nasser was not met until Egypt recognised the People's Republic of China. The then President Eisenhower withdrew US funding of the Aswan Dam and Nasser retaliated by nationalising the Suez Canal Company.

The British and French hatched a plan to 'allow' Israel to invade the Sinai and then intervene. Their major error was to not keep the US informed of their subterfuge. What was planned to be a minor incursion escalated into what became known as the Suez Crisis. The Israelis moved swiftly and ruthlessly and soon a full scale conflict was underway with an Anglo-French invasion force trying to contain the Egyptians. To support this invasion, large air forces and support militia had been deployed to Cyprus and Malta by Britain and France.

Hundreds of lives were lost and many countries were concerned about the escalating hostilities. Eventually Canada led the way to negotiate a peace through the United Nations Emergency Force (UNEF) and the canal reopened on 24 April 1957.

down a bit and the battalion came home. I came home slightly earlier but again I'm jumping the gun a bit.

For the first eighteen months life was hard. We were living in the mountains sending out patrols to monitor police stations because the terrorists thought nothing of attacking these stations and stealing their weapons. In many ways I'm sure these terrorists were being helped by the ethnic police anyway but we were taking over, to at least stop them getting hold of more weapons. British naval destroyers were brought in to do island patrolling to stop any added rearmaments of the terrorists taking place. Our regiment was stationed in a place called Polomedia, just north of the Port of Limassol. Into the port sailed HMS *Diana*, a British destroyer of the 'Daring' class and we took the crew over as our affiliated friends so to speak. This meant that whenever they were in port, for refuelling and restocking – which took about three or four days – they would send us some sailors to join our patrols and as a break, we would send some of our soldiers on board to do watches and so on, sailing around the island on coastal patrol. We also engaged in games and sport: football, hockey, cricket, as and when we could. Their petty officers use to come to our sergeants' mess and we used to have parties together. The officers did the same. Of course there were other ships as well but the *Diana* was our favorite.

After about twelve to fourteen months word got around that the general situation was easing a bit and they were going to allow wives and families to come out; of course all of us were missing our families by now. A purpose built married quarters village was encaged in barbed-wire fencing and guarded. Troops had to go on what was called married quarters guard and patrol around the outskirts: a bit of a bind for the soldiers but nevertheless handy for all the husbands.

So when Enid eventually came out things were improving and we could move about a bit more freely. There was less activity from the terrorists, whereas before you would have got shops and cars being blown up on a regular basis. We had adopted the tactics of pushing the rat back down its hole so to speak: stopping and searching people and cars at check points. Terrorist activity didn't stop but it certainly slowed down.

Once Enid and most of the families had arrived we had a dance in our sergeants' mess in camp, which was of course also surrounded by barbed wire and heavily guarded. The *Diana* was in port and their petty officers came up to join us – there must have been about twenty-five petty officers at this dance and buffet party, with everyone having a good time.

Our President of the Mess Committee (PMC), Jack Howland, was a bit of a character; he said that we'd see these 'jolly jack tars' off in fine style. The sanitary situation in the barracks was that you had deep trench latrines (which meant trenches dug to about 10–15 feet with boarding over the top of them and surrounded by canvas) for use during the day. For night times we use to have what we called the pee bucket at the end of each section of tents, so if you wanted a pee in the night you got out and peed in the bucket. When it was time for the naval guys to leave the PMC got a couple of the sergeants to go and get a few pee buckets and bring them down to the guardroom. The petty officers climbed aboard their transport at the security barrier and someone shouted, 'Are you all on?' and the reply came back 'Yes' so the order was given to lift the barrier. As they started off the PMC ordered the two sergeants to empty the contents of the pee buckets over the sailors. Of course they could do nothing about it as they were on their way back to the ship; the driver had been briefed to 'put his foot down' and not stop till he reached the quay.

That seemed a big joke that we had played on them, not a very nice one I grant you but they got their own back. About three months later we had a warrant officers and sergeants visit to the petty officers' mess on board the *Diana*. They did treat us well; we had bags of food and lots of rum – they must have saved up all their daily rations to provide this. We had games: question and answer games and quizzes and someone had a very small roulette wheel to bet on. We had been there since two o'clock in the afternoon, it was a Sunday, and we were leaving at about 6 p.m. Of course we had all had a lot to drink and we had to leave in a small liberty boat, an outboard, to take us back to port. So we climbd down the ladders into these boats and I'm not joking: they turned the ship's hose on us. We were all in our best kit and they nearly drowned us – a suitable retribution for our antics three months earlier of course. We ought to have known something was going to happen because all the sailors who were there to take us back to port were kitted out in oilskins! Ironically, owing to the rotation of companies, there were only two or three of us who had been at the previous mess do, so a lot of senior NCOs got soaked and had done nothing wrong!

That was some of the lighter side of things. During this period our casualties were not that many; we lost two men by enemy activity when a bomb was detonated by the side of one of our vehicles in the mountains. We also lost five others in motoring accidents, probably caused by the speed they were travelling at. You see, if you were going to be a target you didn't hang about, you put your foot down and got on with it.

We didn't have any regular arrangements. In the camp we had five companies. HQ Company always stayed in HQ, actually in the camp itself. Then we had a company called the 'town patrol company', who lived in the town. In fact they were actually in the Keo Brewery in Limassol. They used to do stop and search in the town, put up barriers and stop cars and things like that, generally just making a nuisance of themselves. We did get one or two 'takes' this way, people being taken away for questioning.

We had four or five in a patrol at night with different patrols in different areas or streets for a month. You were pretty glad when the changeover took place.

One of the companies was on camp duties in the main camp where the HQ was, doing all the guard duties and various other daytime duties to improve the camp. We had another on police stations to ensure that weapons didn't fall into the terrorists' hands and another on copper mines. Copper was blasted out and so we had to escort the explosives and generally control usage to make sure none was left lying around. There were three of these mines with twenty-five men involved each day at any one time.

Cordon and search companies were the two companies usually in cooperation. They would decide on a particular village, having collected intelligence on wanted terrorists. At about 3 o'clock in the morning one company would quietly go and put a tight cordon around the village. A siren was sounded at first light then the other company who made up the search parties would drive into the village and do a house to house search. Anyone trying to escape would run straight into the hands of the surrounding cordon. I can only remember one single person being caught by this method: a fellow who had been 'misbehaving' with a woman from the next village and was trying to get home before his wife woke up. But we kept on doing this month after month after month. I don't know whether they had an informer on the inside because we never knew where we were going until the night before the operation.

All these different activities were for a month at a time then the companies swapped around.

The company on regimental duties in the camp also had to go down to Berengaria Village, which was the name given to the married families' village. They had to help construct it and guard it too. We did have periods as well when we had a company on standby or at ease, as we called it, when they did nothing but play sport and relax.

At the end of my second year I got promoted to colour sergeant (CSgt) just after Enid arrived at the start of 1958 and brought Ian too, who I hadn't seen since he was a few weeks old. I was given leave to go and collect them from the airport and I was able to go right onto the tarmac to meet them. Ian was just starting to walk by this time and there was an RAF officer – this was a military flight – who was supervising disembarkation and luggage pick-up. Ian said to this officer, 'You're not my Daddy,' and then looked at me and said, 'You're my Daddy.' He came toddling across to me and I picked him up and hugged him. The reason Ian could recognise me was because Enid had been showing him my photo every day. When he could speak he kept asking, 'When am I going to see my Daddy?' But I thought it was absolutely remarkable how he came to me and said, 'That's my Daddy.'

Enid spent some time after she arrived bringing me up to speed with Ian's development. She said that at about the same time he had started to take his first tentative steps he had started to listen to what people were saying. She could see that he was starting to pay attention to what she was saying to him and he had started to say 'Mummy' and 'Daddy' and that sort of thing. She said that the funny thing about it was that she'd be out and about in town and people who knew her would stop and enquire after her and the baby. If they asked Ian, 'Well, where's your Daddy then?' he would point skyward and Enid said that they must have thought I'd died and gone to Heaven or something. Of course Enid had told Ian that I'd gone in an aeroplane and he knew that aeroplanes went over the top of him so he'd point up.

In Cyprus things continued to ease off and restrictions relaxed. We had an area of beach which was called 'ladies' mile' sectioned off by barbed-wire with soldiers patrolling it. The wives use to take the families down to the beach while their men were at work. They had daily transport to take them and bring them back. They were well looked after. Of course there was a NAAFI (Navy, Army and Air Force Institutes) shop within the village where they could get all their groceries and everything you could dream of for the house.

We also had a picture house or cinema controlled by the AKC (Army Kinema Corporation). These people weren't actually serving soldiers but they all wore uniforms; they were like a secondary army. We used to go to the pictures quite often. One film we had gone to see was *Fire Down Below* with Robert Mitchum, Jack Lemmon and Rita Hayworth, but we hadn't been sat there for more than ten minutes when there was this enormous bang; the terrorists had bombed our NAAFI. We had to evacuate the cinema and all the men then started to salvage as much as they could from the NAAFI – not the food and stuff, oh no, all the beer cases! Later on proper organisation came in to sort things out – I guess we probably messed up the crime scene. And we never did get to see *Fire Down Below*.

It transpired that a local woman had bought this bomb in between her legs. We had a lot of local people come to work in Berengeria Village: cleaners and workers in the NAAFI and the cinema and such. Of course all these itinerant workers were stopped and searched at the entrance but nobody had picked up on this and she had left the bomb behind when she went home.

Now the families weren't allowed out on their own unless escorted. So the families' village was their little world.

As colour sergeant (I was now wearing three stripes and a crown) I'd come off the platoon activities and I was now controlling the company's stores so I became the company quartermaster sergeant (CQMS): a senior rank to a sergeant. In this position I was mainly responsible for goods and chattels – everything to do with the clothing of soldiers about the place and the equipment they needed. Each company had a CQMS and the regiment had a regimental quartermaster sergeant. He was higher than a Company Sergeant Major, in the warrant officer class. But as colour sergeants we're still in the sergeants' class.

So I became CQMS for Support Company where my MMGs were. We had put aside all our MMGs because they weren't required; in fact thinking back I can't remember if the company bought any with us. We were renamed the ferret platoon – they used to go out in semi-armoured vehicles called 'ferrets' to do all their patrolling, whereas most of the other companies would be transported to destination and patrol on foot.

I was now constantly in camp, except when I was visiting the company at the out of camp locations: restocking ammo, petrol and food, delivering mail and so on. A little freer on time I suppose but I did get caught up for sergeants' mess duties. I was made catering member for the sergeants' mess: the one who selected the menus and told the chefs what to cook and what not to cook. That was one of the more onerous job that I didn't particularly like – the members got plenty of Yorkshire puddings, I can tell you!

Generally speaking, through the whole island, things had gone off the boil. We got the odd little flare-ups from time to time but nothing serious. So on the sporting front our battalion football team could play other battalions throughout the area: Episcopi, and to Akrotiri to play against the RAF. We also went across the island to Nicosia and down to Larnaka to play their teams. Movement was safer now so we could get out and about more with our families to a certain degree and people started buying cars. Things got easier.

As things go I had to lose my crown from my stripes because the army was thinning out and the 2nd battalion of the King's Royal Rifle Corp (KRRC) had been disbanded. They had been serving in Mogadishu in Somalia at the time and had people who had not been abroad very long who were transferring them to our regiment in Cyprus. Amongst them were two senior colour sergeants (CQMSs) and because I was not substantive, I had to come down to Sergeant again. My company commander, Major David Wood, was most sympathetic and said it wouldn't be long before I'd get my CQMS again. Now this demotion wasn't like before when I had lost my sergeant's stripe when I chose to come home from Egypt – in that case I moved to a different unit. This time it was embarrassing; one day you're a colour sergeant, with some kind of authority, and the next you're reduced to a sergeant again. The soldiers don't understand the implications and may think you'd done something wrong which was not true.

Indeed there was another fella, my mate Joe Haydon, who was in a similar position. He had been the officers' mess caterer: a colour sergeant appointment. Like me he wasn't substantive and so he had to come down too. That did however mean that in sympathy with our situation the CO and the Infantry Records Office agreed that we could get posted. Joe got posted as PSI to the Regiment's TA unit in Oxford and I got posted as a Drill and Weapons Training Instructor to Sandhurst.

There were thirty-six people up for seven posts at Sandhurst and I came out second from top. The other fella that beat me was also a Green Jacket from my battalion, Sgt. Jim Norgate, so I didn't mind so much. Jim, was to go on to complete his 22 years and retired as a regimental sergeant major (RSM).

During our tour of duty in Cyprus, Harold Wilson the Prime Minister of the time had approved a reorganisation of the armed forces. The army was the worst hit, the infantry in particular; regiments were disbanded, others merged. My regiment, the Oxf. & Bucks., were taken out of the Light Infantry Brigade and put into a new brigade, together with the Rifle

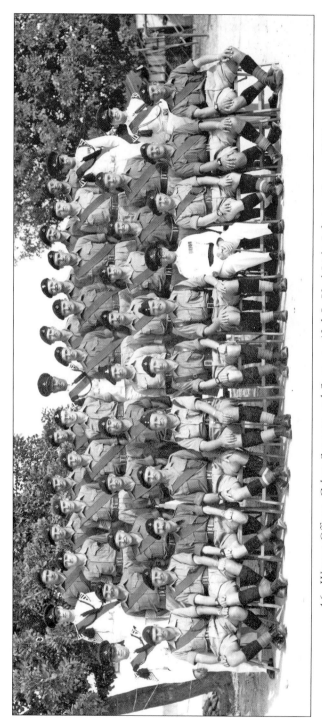

16. *Warrant Officers, Colour Sergeants and Sergeants 43rd & 52nd Light Infantry, Cyprus 1957. (Last Sergeant's Mess photo of Oxf. & Bucks, before we became 1st Green Jackets)*

Brigade and the King's Royal Rifle Corps, now to be titled the Green Jacket Brigade. From now on we were 1st Green Jackets 43rd and 52nd effective from 1 April 1958. But we were not badged and uniformed until much later in the year. So when I went to Sandhurst, I was a Green Jacket.

# Chapter 10

# Sergeant to CSM, Sandhurst as Green Jacket (1959–62)

O FF I WENT BACK TO ENGLAND to Sandhurst, initially to attend a selection course that was only going to allow seven people to pass. As I said I came second and the post was for three years. I was posted to Burma Company in Victory College, training recruits who had come straight into the army as potential officers. This was different to what I had done in Strensall where I was training potential national service officers – these cadets were already destined to be regular officers. The most prestigious cadet to pass through Sandhurst whilst I was there was Prince Michael, who was in Victory College but in Normandy Company.

Enid had come back from Cyprus with Ian and gone to stay with her Mum and Dad whilst I went on the Sandhurst selection course. Obviously there were no married quarters or anything like that until it had been confirmed that I'd been selected – I would have been RTU'd (Returned To Unit) if I had failed – but that was not the case as I passed and we got a married quarter just inside the Academy grounds. Before I had completed this course sadly Enid's father had died in hospital from lung cancer.

It was quite a prestigious job I suppose. Up to that point it had been nearly seven years since I had first made sergeant, doing one thing or another. So I went to Sandhurst as a sergeant and a year after I'd been there I was promoted to colour sergeant again, substantive immediately, through the Infantry Records Office which overrode any regimental dealings. My annual report said that I was eligible for substantive colour sergeant and recommended that I should be promoted to that rank. I got the Company Stores job for Burma Company. This meant that I still did the normal instructing of cadets but I had to look after the stores as well.

A rather unusual thing in the Academy was that all permanent staff and cadets were issued with bicycles. These were necessary for such was the acreage of the Royal Military Academy (RMA) grounds that without a bike, you might not get to the next point of instruction in time, particularly if you needed a change of clothing, for example from drill smart uniform to weapon training denims.

Sandhurst was a good career move for me as it introduced me to all the cadets passing through the college and going to various regiments. In later life I would meet up with officers that I had trained and it was the same with the staff. The staff was manned equally by different line regiments and Guards consisting of five regiments: Coldstream, Grenadier, Irish, Welsh and Scots. Together with the mounted Guards, such as the Blues and Royals and the Life Guards, these made up the household division. This division was mainly responsible for public duties which included guarding the palaces, public places, Windsor Castle and so on. All these different regiments were mixed up between colleges and companies.

The instructors at Sandhurst, particularly on the drill side, were mainly guardsmen, and the sergeants from the line regiments did things like instructing mainly in weapon training, shooting and grenade throwing. The principal person on the Guards' side was the Academy Sergeant Major (ASM) albeit he was a warrant officer class one (WO1). In this position he was No. 1 soldier in the army if you like. Whilst I was at Sandhurst the ASM was John Lord, a Grenadier – he had been a prisoner of war (POW) and had a reputation for discipline. In his POW camp he had made all the soldiers drill and line up in front of the Germans to show them their spirits weren't broken and he got a commendation for that. It was a real pleasure serving under him. He was respected by everyone.

Whilst at Sandhurst I got to know a lot about the Guards and got to know a lot of them personally too, not only the other NCO ranks like me but officers as well. Also serving at the Academy was RSM Tom Taylor, who had been my platoon sergeant at Sennelager – we became friends and Enid and I socialised with Tom and his wife, May.

During my term at Sandhurst Enid became pregnant again and produced our second son, Graham. Enid wasn't feeling too well but didn't know what was the matter. She went to the doctor and he said, 'Didn't you realise you were pregnant?'

Enid said, 'I can't be pregnant,' and the doctor asked 'Why's that?'

She replied, 'My husband promised me we wouldn't have any more children.'

The doctor smiled and said, 'Mrs Lawless, the number of women who have sat there and said that to me is countless.'

And so she had our Graham in Louise-Margaret Maternity Hospital in Aldershot on 19 January 1961, three days after I became thirty-one.

We had an old fashioned married quarter but it did have three floors and four bedrooms so when our relatives from the north wanted to come and visit we could put them up quite easily. Enid's Mum must have spent a least two of the three years we were at Sandhurst staying with us. With two young kids Gladys was a terrific help to both Enid and me, particularly when Graham was born. I had to go and do night exercises and such things as that so it was great for Enid not to be left on her own.

One time, on the occasion of the Sandhurst summer ball, we were able to put up five of Enid's family. This was a rather grand black tie affair with all the officers' families being there. The Assistant Quartermaster of the Academy, Lt. Don Truluck, was a Green Jacket and he had invited us to his table. I was going to meet him again in later years – life in the army was like that. Shortly after we had got there and found our seats Enid went to the toilet – I have noticed that when one woman goes a whole group follow. This time one of Enid's nieces came back and said, 'My auntie Enid has done something to her leg.' Well in fact Enid had tripped on the stairs and twisted her ankle. I was trying to persuade her to let me take her home but she was adamant that she was staying. Some of the comments coming from the 'lesser mortals' were things like 'She's only been here five minutes and she's bloody drunk already.' Enid was furious because she didn't drink. Despite her discomfort she stayed until the end.

Sgt. Jim Norgate and his wife Madge from my own regiment were also at the ball and joined our group. Having finished his military service he got a job with a large retail outlet – sadly, at far too young an age, he had a heart attack and died. However I am still on Christmas card terms with Madge.

Another thing that happened whilst we were at Sandhurst was that I bought my first car, a Morris 1000 I think, and learnt to drive in the Academy grounds. I passed my driving test with the army after a few lessons. Earlier in my career I had driven heavy goods vehicles and suchlike as part of my job but never got a licence – I just got on with the job. Now I sent off through the Motor Transport Office and got my first driving licence. My very first drive on a British road was to take my family up to Rotherham to see our respective families. This was a bit different from driving on Cypriot roads on patrol but I did it anyway.

Then blow me, one term before my three years was up in post I was promoted to substantive Company Sergeant Major (CSM), WO2 (warrant officer class two). This meant I lost my stripes but got my crown back on the bottom of my sleeve. As there was no position for my rank at the Academy I had to leave but I had almost finished my tour of duty anyway.

I played cricket and football for the Academy sergeants' mess side. One particular cricket game I remember was when we were playing the Brighton Police down in Brighton. I was a bowler and got my one and only hat-trick and I shan't forget that.

Whilst at Sandhurst, in addition to it being a good career posting, I also had the opportunity to become a parachutist. I say parachutist rather than paratrooper because I had no intention of joining the Parachute Regiment, for which the course was intended. Selected cadets at Sandhurst, usually the ones who were going to the Paras or SAS, undertook a course in parachute jumping, consisting of eight jumps over a period of four to six weeks. These courses were repeated up to three times in a year. Each course consisted of no more than twenty personnel, of which two were volunteers from the staff. I volunteered and was selected. As a Colour Sergeant I was looked upon as the leader of our group. All the instruction took place at the RAF Training Centre in Abingdon near Oxford, where we all stayed during the week and went home at weekends. After ten days of gym training, getting fit and practising landing rolls, learning flight manoeuvres and parachute control, it was time for our first drop. This was to be at a place called Weston-on-the-Green near Oxford, jumping from a balloon, or rather from a basket suspended from a balloon. We went up six at a time with an instructor.

At six thirty on a lovely summer's morning, the balloon started to rise and the ground fell away below us. Everywhere was quiet, no one was talking – a few tried to whistle through dry lips. Up we went, higher and higher and it started to look rather daunting. I noticed a few trickles of water were starting to appear on the floor of the basket. At the height of 800 feet, the limit we were told we were going to jump from, we stopped. The instructor gave us all our last instructions; we carried out our final kit checks and prepared to go, one by one. You know what's coming: yes, as the most senior there, it was me first. I exited through the rear of the basket, with the balloon swaying just above our heads. Holding the jump position, I dropped longer than I had anticipated; it seemed ages, although I'm sure it was only a few seconds. I'd just convinced myself that the chute wasn't going to open when there was a loud crack and I stopped in my descent, momentarily, then the parachute started to blossom out and there I was swinging and falling slowly under this lovely canopy. I quickly remembered all the things that I had been taught, adjusted my harness and grabbed the chute control tabs. I floated down but quicker than I thought, the ground came up to meet me and I had no time at all to carry out my landing drills and landed in a heap. The Officer Controller on the ground, who had been bellowing out instructions to me from when I'd been within earshot, asked first if I was all right and then said it was the worst landing he'd ever seen and that I had to kit up again and do another drop. It turned out this wasn't a punishment but a part of the programme; we all had to do a second drop. Although we had gone out of the side of the basket on the first jump, we now had to drop through the floor for our second. I must say that there was a certain amount of pleasure with the second attempt. The next three jumps were from a plane, two from the side and one from the tail. The last three were also from a plane but this time with full kit and in battle formation, one after the other in quick succession. These last jumps were also at night and into water. All my group passed and were awarded the parachute cloth badge to be sewn onto the left sleeve of our battledress. It was an altogether great experience.

I thought that when I finished my tour at Sandhurst I was going to go back to my regiment who were now in Warminster, bearing in mind that I hadn't been back with them for quite some time. However it transpired that there were two guys of my seniority who had been promoted like me to WO2 and they were acting CSMs within the regiment. Unlike me however they were not substantive, which meant that if I had gone back to the regiment one of them would have to go back to CQMS. Now all right, it had happened to me so why shouldn't it happen to one of them? However it was slightly different here because there weren't many CQMSs in the regiment and hence no position for a 'demoted' CSM to take up, or that's how the CO looked at it anyway. And that's how he explained it to me and said that if I was patient enough to be away from the regiment for another tour, then I would be coming back and looking at something maybe more than CSM so it would be to my advantage not to go back to the regiment at that time. He explained that there was a job which was overseas in Kenya working as a Permanent Staff Instructor (PSI) to the Kenya Regiment. This was a regiment of all white Kenyans formed to produce senior NCOs and officers for the King's African Rifles. They had always been under British management. This was a very strong position for me and an addition to my learning curve. It paid at overseas rates which were far in excess of being at home. So knowing that Enid would enjoy travelling abroad I took it, and off I went to Kenya.

CHAPTER 11

# CSM (PSI), Kenya
# (1962–63)

I HAD MY CAR TAKEN to Kenya by the Royal Navy. One of the permanent staff officers at Sandhurst, who was a naval officer attached to the Royal Military Academy Sandhurst (RMAS), made all the arrangements for me. Even though he was an officer and I was a CSM we got on quite well because we both played in the cricket team at Sandhurst – so here's another example as how my sporting exploits helped me.

After signing off from Sandhurst, in May 1962, we handed over our married quarter and moved to Enid's mother's house in Rotherham. My movement orders said that I had to report to the Kenya Regiment by 1 July 1962 which meant that I had five weeks' leave. During this time I had to go to the regimental HQ in Winchester and collect my tropical clothing which, with plenty of time on hand, I did towards the end of May.

I had to stay in the sergeants' mess overnight and was royally entertained by the 'living-in members'. I collected my gear from the QM the next day and went back home to Yorkshire. When I got home Enid had already enrolled Ian in the local infants' school in Rotherham. Unbeknown to me she had opened a telegram from the Kenya Regiment that said that I was needed as soon as possible but as the regiment were at annual camp I had to go by myself, leaving the family to come out later, which might be as much as three months afterwards. Enid said Ian was not going without schooling for three months. In the event it was the end of June before I set off owing to a cock-up with my travel documents, but I arrived in Nairobi on 30 June 1962 and called into the battalion HQ in Nairobi just to make my mark and let them know I had arrived. I was billeted in a hotel in Nyeri, just north of Nairobi.

I was met in Nyeri by WO2 John McGrady, the PSI whom I was to replace. He looked after me and got me settled in. The next day he was taking me up to meet the company commander at his farm. I spent that evening and most of the night getting all my uniform and equipment clean and tidy; getting my boots shined up smartly and my bush hat, which I'd never worn before, nicely bent up one side with the cap badge on. I thought I looked quite smart. When the PSI turned up the next morning to take me out to meet the OC, he wasn't dressed up, he was just in mufti. I wasn't sure about this and the Land Rover he had was a scruffy as anything too. I put that down to the state of the roads because they weren't a tarmac surface, just hard clay. Well, we went miles out into the country. The OC's house was a low wooden bungalow type of building and to get to it we drove down a big long drive that was about three quarters of a mile long. The OC was Major 'Rogue' Barcas, a smashing fella who had previous been in the Durham Light Infantry before he had emigrated to Kenya with his wife Peggy. Now, remember I had just left Sandhurst, the Mecca of army discipline and drill where you had to be as shiny as a button stick all the time. The Major had on a pair of slippers and a scruffy old shirt hanging outside his shorts. I clicked my heels together and saluted and his very first words to me as his new CSM were 'You can fucking well cut that out.' Well, I was flabbergasted.

He said, 'We don't go in for that sort of thing here. What's your name?'

I said, 'Company Sergeant Major Lawless, Sir.'

He said, 'No, no not that bullshit, what is your first name?'

I replied, 'Peter,' and he said, 'Well, that's what you are then, Peter. My name is Rogue. You will call me Sir when there's anyone else about but other than that I'm Rogue.'

Well, what a difference from leaving Sandhurst and arriving in Kenya. Afterwards I got used to this but this was my introduction to how this Territorial Army was run. And it was like that all the time I was in Kenya. They were keen enough and got on and did the job all right but they had no, what I called, solid discipline. But no matter what I thought about it privately, it did work.

We sat down to some tea and finished up having a beer and Rogue said to me, 'How soon can you have your working clothes on?'

I said to him, 'I thought I already had them on, Sir,' and he said, 'Look, cut the Sir out, will you, you're making me feel embarrassed.'

Well, I really couldn't handle this at first, it was all so odd. The other PSI in the meantime was laughing his socks off because he knew what would happen when he saw me come out of the hotel to start with. Of course he wasn't going to warn me, he just wanted to see how I'd react: the bugger.

So I asked the OC when he wanted me and he said, 'Tomorrow

morning. I'll come and pick you up and we'll go out to the training area,'
to annual camp.

I said, 'OK, fine,' and he said to the other PSI, 'And you can bugger off
back to Nairobi.' That was my introduction to the Kenya regiment –
marvellous!

I found it a bit strange at first but I soon settled into their ways. We
quickly got the company into first class order. In the Nanyuki area they
had miles and miles of fields and forest where we used to do exercises and
so on and so forth and this helped tremendously. Not long after I'd arrived
one of the lads was late for a morning muster parade. We used to have this
at 8:30 every morning but this lad was about half an hour late. So I, being
the disciplinarian, put him on a charge and put him in front of the OC. I
explained that he had strolled up half an hour late to muster parade and the
OC said to him, 'Right, well, don't do that again. Case dismissed.'

After the lad had left I said, 'Look, Sir, how can you expect to have
discipline amongst the blokes if you don't actually punish them for doing
wrong? That bloke was blatantly half an hour late. Now he just thinks he
can turn up any time he wants.' I carried on, 'Either he's in the army or
he's not. You've got to have some sort of discipline. How would it be if
someone's coming over the top, they're rushing toward you with a weapon
and you turn to find that bloke's not there because he's not bothered to
turn up? It's not on.'

'Well,' he said, 'I would have punished him, but what can I do?'

I said, 'You could have confined him to camp, for instance, and stopped
him going into town to get tanked up with his mates.'

He replied, 'I would have done but I'm borrowing his tractor next week
and don't want to do anything to upset him.' This was quite true; most of
the blokes were farmers as well as being in the TA. So that's the way they
used to work in the Kenya regiment – I got used to it in the end. We all
settled down and there were no great problems after that.

On the second weekend that I was there I flew down to Mombasa, on
the coast, to pick up my car. Luckily for me one of my company
lieutenants, Gilfred Powys, was a platoon commander of the Coast Platoon
and owned a tobacco farm and had his own plane. My car had been
collected by the Coast Platoon. Well, I'd flown home from Cyprus and
flown here to Kenya and been quite encouraged by flying. But flying in
this small plane was something else – really exhilarating – particularly the
way Gilfred flew, skimming through the tops of trees, diving to look at

rhinos! I'm sure I went through the whole gambit of emotions – what a flight.

Eventually Enid did come out and she brought the two bairns with her. Ian was nearly six now and Graham was about two and a half. We got a married quarter initially close to the camp out by the airfield in Nyeri, where I reported each day. The blokes had their own work to do and their own farms to take care of during the day, so they would just turn up one evening a week for drill and weapons training and then again at the weekends for more training.

At the end of annual camp we got moved to where the annual camp had been, in Nanyuki, which was something like twenty or thirty miles north of Nyeri. It was mostly under canvas but there were a few buildings and there were plenty of deep trench latrines. It was agreed that this would make a good Company HQ and we moved there. We set up camp, built one or two more wooden buildings, some more latrines and more solid accommodation and D Company HQ settled there.

Then Enid and the kids moved with me to Nanyuki to an old planter's home. It was a nice big bungalow with three bedrooms and all made of

*17. Trophies on the veranda at Nanyuki*

wood, mounted on concrete pillars with steps up to the veranda in the front, where a number of trophy horns were hung. Out of the kitchen window we had a marvellous view of Mount Kenya – always snow-capped; this was a magnificent sight whilst having your cornflakes.

The previous owners had emigrated to South Africa because there were rumours that Kenya was going to get its independence from the Commonwealth and things might not be the same after that. In fact there were already lotteries being held where white owners' ranches were being apportioned out to native Kenyans.

When we moved in there was still some animosity between the whites and the locals with regard to the farm ownership. We use to have all sorts of queer people come and look down our drive. We had to be very careful about what sort of impression we gave these people. To make sure we were kept safe we got given this dog by a family who were going back to the UK, a lovely black retriever called Blackie. I guess this dog had been trained to hate black people. When the postman used to come he would shout, 'Memsahib, memsahib,' up the drive, 'post, post!' He wouldn't walk up to the bungalow because of the dog, Kenyans couldn't stand them.

We had a *shamba* boy (a gardener) whose name was Kararua. He wasn't that old, probably about twenty years of age. We also had a house boy, who used to do the cleaning and occasionally a little bit of cooking but not too much, because Enid needed to keep her hand in. However he did all the washing up and that sort of thing and took the kids for walks. We had a good acre of ground and a stream running along the bottom of the property as well which was rather pretty. After that it was bush, not too thick but nevertheless a bit thicker than Sherwood Forest.

We settled in. There was one incident with Graham whilst we were there. I was at work, up at the camp we'd built. Enid called me to say could I get home quick because Graham had got in the way of a column of red soldier ants. He was covered in them and crying and Enid was panicking. Fortunately our house boy knew what to do. Outside we had a great big water butt for watering the garden which was always kept full and he got hold of Graham and dumped him in the water butt to wash the ants off him. He asked Enid to get some vinegar, which luckily we had, and he poured this all over Graham. The vinegar obviously killed the ants because any that were left fell off after that. Luckily Graham was all right even though he had little red bite marks all over him. We did get him to the doctor's and he gave us some cream but he was OK. Graham still talks about that incident today. And we pull his leg and call him the ant man!

One time Ian wanted to go fishing in the stream. I had to go with him because you never knew what might appear out of the jungle. There were monkeys and parakeets and other animals so we had to keep an eye on him. Although it wasn't very deep it was quite a fast flowing stream so we did need to be careful. Anyway there he was fishing with a great long branch with a piece of string tied at one end and a toy fire engine on the other to see what he could catch. With the weight of the toy and the flow of the stream Ian ended up falling in. So I, being a crafty so and so and knowing that I was now going to be in trouble with Enid, told Ian, 'When we get back and your Mum asks what happened you tell her that the dog knocked you in.' So that's what we told Enid went we got back. And so she always believed that the dog knocked Ian in the stream. We laughed about that in future years.

I had been given a company Land Rover and driver and I used to pick Ian up from school each day as this coincided with me leaving the office. After a while Enid said to me, 'Ian's not very happy with you. He wants to know whether you could stop a little further up the road so that he can come to you.'

I said, 'Why?'

Enid explained that people were laughing at him because when I went to get him I'd shout, 'Come on, herry up, get on with it.' They'd heard of hurry up but not 'herry' up, so they'd laugh trying to get their heads around my language. I thought, cheeky little bugger.

When we were talking about it later Ian said, 'But Dad, you also say other funny things. You say giraffe.'

I said, 'Of course I do.'

He said, 'It's not, it's a 'girarffe [accent on the 'a' in the middle].'

I said, 'Who's told you that?'

Ian replied that everyone pronounced it that way. So I said, 'Well, the next time they say anything to you, you tell them that as far as I'm concerned there's only one 'r' in giraffe and not two!'

One day we were going into town, Nanyuki, to pick Ian up from school and because of the heat all the windows were down (there was no air conditioning in those days). All of a sudden the dog dived over my shoulder and out of my window. It did three or four somersaults on the road because we were doing a fair speed, recovered and pinned a native bloke up against a tree. Well, the poor fellow was cowering up against the tree with his hands up over his head in a surrender position. Anyway we eventually managed to call the dog off and get him back in the car.

It was a good posting for me but it was a man's country. Everything was about hunting, shooting and fishing. As a PSI I was expected to be involved in the organisation of many local events. Once a year there was a major polo tournament and I was immediately grabbed to help organise it. This involved clearing the ground where the matches were to take place, and making sure there were sufficient stands for the crowd and sufficient facilities for the horses. I also had to organise a bar and get the beer in from the local *duccas* (local shops). These were the sort of things I got involved with outside my main army responsibilities.

I also became an honorary member of the Mount Kenya Safari Club which was a really top class club where all the American film stars always stayed when they came to Kenya on safari. Later on Enid and I were able to go there and have some good times when we visited. The Nanyuki Sports Club was like a social club; most of the families used to gather there, mostly white, I might add. I was also put onto the committee in that club because of being PSI of the Kenya Regiment and I helped to run the hockey team and organise one or two outings, which included, for one of my Company's training weekends, a trip to the top of Mount Kenya.

Climbing Mount Kenya at 17,057 ft was not as difficult as it might seem and I was very excited about it. We didn't have all the gear like crampons and such for ice climbing as you can walk up it. Lenana is one of the peaks up there, named after a Masai chieftain, just by the side of a big glacier and that's where we were heading. We set off on the Friday evening having met up at our HQ in Nanyuki. We drove to the Warden's Cottage at 7,900 ft – this was home to the park's senior wardens until 1998 – just outside the entrance to the National Park and stayed there the night. We had a bar on one of the vehicles so were able to have a few drinks that night. We went up the Naro Moru route, Naro Moru being a village on the road between Nanyuki and Nyeri which I'd driven past a few times. We used pack horses which belonged to the Kenyan army to carry all our tentage, cooking utensils and food. Although it was my company that were doing this walk our Adjutant Christopher Adami had elected to come with us because like all of us he was very excited about having the chance to climb Mount Kenya.

So we set out the next day, Saturday, and walked to the metrological station at 10,000 ft to have a meal. We could have stopped here because there were some properly constructed bunkhouses but we wanted to push on because of the limited time we had; the TA blokes had to be back at work on Monday. So we set off again and arrived at Mackinder's Camp at 13,778 ft below point Lenana at dusk at around 6 to 6:30 p.m. We put tents up here although there were some buildings there too.

It was interesting to see that even at this altitude there were small animals called rock hyrax scurrying about between the rocks. These were a bit like small rabbits. Another interesting thing was that I hadn't realised that a lot of my blokes had never touched snow before. They'd obviously seen it from afar but never been near enough to grab hold of it. They were just like kids running about in the snow and throwing snowballs at each other.

Before we bedded down for the night we were also issued with tablets to help us sleep and we were warned about breathing difficulties due to the altitude.

The next morning we did the last leg of about 2,000 ft up the glacier to Point Lenana at 16,355 ft which is the furthest you can actually walk up Mount Kenya. Beyond this you need to do some serious climbing with ropes and such to reach the two highest peaks: Batian at 17,058 ft and

*18. Point Lenana at 16,355 ft*

*19. Thompsons Falls, Nanyuki*

Nelion at 17,022 ft. We all managed to get out on to the glacier but couldn't hang around because we needed to start our descent.

The descent was easier than the climb up and having had one stop on the way down we got back about 9 o'clock in the evening in time for the vehicles to pick us up and take us back to Nanyuki.

The blokes got paid for the weekend plus their expenses as they were volunteers, although, I have to say, that they never did get paid any expenses because this always went on their bar bills.

Another little town close to Nanyuki was Thomson's Falls where some of our TA people lived. Enid and I got friendly with one family in particular, Pete and Ann Smith. They had two small kids like us and we often used to visit them. Now Thomson's Falls is very aptly named because it is right by a massive waterfall, a really splendid sight, and people used to come from far and wide to see it.

Pete worked on a farm owned by another Peter, Peter Overdyke. Like most whites in Kenya these guys had South African origins. Anyway one day both Peters asked me to go on a shooting trip with them. They produced the game rifles which were different from our army rifles and we

*20. First blood*

went off to shoot deer: 'tommy' buck – Thompson gazelles – and the odd impala was the idea. All these animals ran wild as there were no wild life reserves or anything like that at the time. However my first kill was a buffalo. What a grand day out.

The regiment had a major exercise right out in the wilds, miles away from anywhere over a massive big training area. Two companies were the enemy and the rest of the battalion were trying to occupy a certain area which was held by the 'enemy'. Everyone in the regiment was given various tasks to perform and they were left to their own devices – all the TA volunteers had to occupy their proper positions as they would do if there were no PSIs or other training staff around to help them. The company PSIs were umpires – they wore red armbands and made evaluation notes throughout the exercise, except in my case: I was seconded to Gilfred Powys and we were to act as an enemy aeroplane that was protecting the enemy area from above. We had flour bombs and would dive down low over the ground and I would drop bombs on anything that we thought looked suspicious – it was really exciting and I enjoyed flying with Gilfred.

*21. Gilfred's plane with my two kids*

As an aside, I must add that Gilfred took Enid and the kids on a flying safari and they loved every minute of it!

The equator runs straight through the middle of Kenya, between Nyeri, where I lived where I first arrived, and Nanyuki and there is a great big sign there to advertise that fact.

There was a pub nearby – I think they called it the Silverbeck Inn – that had been built right on the equator. There was a metal strip nailed across the bar and you could sip a pint of beer with one foot in the northern hemisphere and the other in the southern hemisphere. It has since burnt down and been rebuilt as a more upmarket hotel.

A typically funny incident involved our *shamba* boy, Kararua. Toward the end of September, beginning of October, the rainy season started. First of all you had the light rains and then you got the heavy rains. We were fascinated because it nearly always rained at about 4 o'clock in the afternoon and went on till about 8 or 9 o'clock at night and then stopped. It was just like someone was timing it and turning the tap on and off. Anyway, towards the end of September my garden was drying up and so I said to Kararua, 'Listen, I want the garden watered today; get the hose pipe

*22. Astride the Equator*

and get on with it. If I come home and you haven't done it there will be trouble,' and off I went. As I was driving home at 4 or 5 o'clock it had started to rain. Well, as I pulled up I could see this bloke standing in the middle of the lawn watering the garden with the rain pouring down all around him. I said, 'Get inside, you silly bugger!' I had told him to water the garden and that is what he was going to do despite the rain.

During this season the rains would get heavier and heavier and fill the storm drains down the side of the roads. These were massive concrete ditches which were needed to be able to carry away the huge amount of rainwater to prevent the area flooding.

I talked earlier about the locals' concerns over Kenya gaining its independence; well, in the end we had to pack up and leave because it happened. What the authorities did was to encourage Africans and Asians to join the Kenya regiment to try to keep the regiment alive because under independence there was no way the Kenyans were going to have a white army. And although we did get some natives joining it wasn't successful and in the end the regiment was put into a kind of suspended state and everyone went back to where they had come from; in Enid's and my case that was the UK. So my time in Kenya lasted only just over a year. We had a massive parade through Nairobi with best kit and everything to close down the regiment.

As is the case throughout my army life I was always bumping into people that I had worked with before. In Kenya this happened to be Derek Hornblower. You will remember Derek was a platoon sergeant in Lüneburg in the same company as me when I first joined the army. We had also served together in Oxford and Cyprus. Six months before we closed down Derek turned up to be PSI RSM of the Kenya regiment.

However now we all had to get posted away from Kenya. We were paid by the Kenyan government and not by the British army and I think we must have been under some sort of contract; indeed, I was signed up for a three year tour of duty. So I ended up being paid a lump sum of money by the Kenyan government and in my case it was quite a lot, something like £1,500. It was a good chunk of money to put in your pocket at that time – we had a few good parties on that when we got home.

I must have put about two stone of weight on whilst I was in Kenya because of the hospitality of the Kenyans. If you visited anyone you would immediately be offered a beer and before you knew it you were on your seventh cold beer and no longer able to drive home. I'd therefore get my driver to come and get me.

I enjoyed my time in Kenya, and I know Enid and the kids did too, but all good things come to an end. We had a jolly good sending off in Nairobi from most of the Kenya Regiment and around sixty people who were in my company, including the CO, Rogue Barkus, and one or two of the other guys I had got friendly with.

When I left Kenya I left my car behind. In truth the Kenya roads had made quite a mess of it: not so great a mess that you couldn't drive it but it wasn't worth bringing home.

I shouldn't leave this chapter without mentioning the Kenya Regiment Association that was formed by groups of ex-Kenya Regiment members when the regiment was 'mothballed'. Many left because of the troubles that were predicted to follow Kenya's independence. They left for New Zealand, Australia, North America/Canada; a large number went to South Africa and plenty came to the UK. I was and still am a member and even to this day I go to Kenya Regiment Association lunches and dinners, which I enjoy immensely. The British Association is grouped with Europe and North America and is called the Kenya Regiment Association of Europe and North America (KRAENA).

CHAPTER 12

# Local RSM, Borneo
# (1963–64)

EVENTUALLY IT WAS DECIDED that the rumours were true and that Kenya was going to get its independence. This meant that the British element of the Kenyan Regiment would have to be found jobs elsewhere or go home because the regiment was going to be disbanded. Actually they weren't really disbanded but rather put into suspended animation which as I write this, they are still in today.

We were given notice because Independence Day was not going to happen immediately, so the authorities started going back to the records office to find out where we could all be posted to. I found out that I was going to be local RSM, which was again a promotion, in HQ 99 Gurkha Infantry Brigade Group who were at that time on active service in Brunei and Borneo. They were there because there had been an incursion by the Indonesians, known as the Brunei Rebellion. Derek Hornblower was being posted to 1 Green Jackets, our old regiment. They were stationed in Penang and on active service in Borneo.

Enid, the boys and I flew home from Kenya to the UK together in early July. Interestingly this was the first time that we had all travelled to or from a posting overseas together. All our bits and pieces had been sent home ahead of us by military freight.

The details surrounding my posting to Brunei weren't very clear; no time or movement instructions had been given. We went to stay with Enid's mother but blimey, I was only back a week before I got notice from the Royal Green Jackets' HQ in Winchester that I needed to go to a place near Aldershot where there was a Gurkha Battalion so that I could attend a course to learn a little Gurkhali. Well, this was a language I'd never heard of but never mind, if I had to learn it to speak to the soldiers I'd do it, although as I understood it the Gurkha soldiers did know a limited amount of English, so I wasn't all that fussed about it. So off I went leaving Enid and the kids with her mother.

I went to do this ten-day course and then I carried on to the depot at Winchester and had to get another load of kit which included battledress

85

The northern part of the island of Borneo was composed of three British territories: the colonies of Sarawak and North Borneo (later renamed Sabah) and the protectorate of the Sultanate of Brunei. In 1929 oil was discovered near Seria and the Shell Petroleum Company concession provided the Sultanate with a huge income.

Between 1959 and 1962, the United Kingdom, Malaya, Singapore, Sabah and Sarawak were involved in negotiations to form a new Malaysian Federation. However, the Philippines and particularly Indonesia opposed any move towards unification of North Borneo and Sarawak with the new federation.

The Brunei Rebellion broke out on 8 December 1962. The rebels began co-ordinated attacks on the oil town of Seria (targeting the Shell oil installations) and on police stations and government facilities around the protectorate. The rebels tried to capture the Sultan of Brunei, seize the oil fields and take European hostages. The Sultan escaped and asked for British help. He received British and Gurkha troops from Singapore. On 16 December, British Far Eastern Command claimed that all major rebel centres had been occupied, and on 17 April 1963, the rebel commander was captured and the rebellion ended.

of a greyish colour which the Gurkhas wore. This had all been ordered from Ordnance in preparation for my posting.

At the end of August I flew to Brunei and again I went by myself because there were no married quarters available, although there was one in the making; I had to go ahead anyway. I was to go via Brigade HQ in Singapore from where I'd go across to the Brigade element in Brunei. During the few days I was in Brigade HQ they told me that there was a married quarter available so they would raise all the appropriate travel documents so that Enid and the kids could come out and join me as soon as possible.

In the meantime I left for Brunei and met the Brigadier and the HQ staff and got to know all the people I was going to be working with. This included the Gurkha Company Sergeant Major who was my sort of contemporary although I was an RSM and he was only a CSM. This of course made me the boss over the whole of the sergeants' mess. For the first time I found myself running the sergeants' mess as well as carrying out my other duties and responsibilities. There were a number of British elements in HQ: clerical staff, drivers, office staff and various other jobs, all under my authority, and an almost all British signals squadron.

I'd only been in Brunei about a week when Enid arrived in Singapore and the powers that be said that I needed to go back and settle my family in, which I thought was really great. The journey between Brunei and Singapore at that time was by ferry to an island called Labuan where there was a good class civil airport and then by air to Singapore. The authorities in Brunei were building an airfield but it wasn't finished yet.

*23. Ian and Graham with their amah, Lim*

I got back to Singapore and settled Enid into our quarter and helped her sort out a schools for Ian (Graham wasn't quite school age yet). We also were entitled to an amah who helped Enid with the house and kids. Her name was Lim and she made a great curry!

I then returned to the brigade in Brunei. I stayed there for a good six months and during that time I did a hell of a lot of visiting battalions with the Brigadier and the HQ staff. We had three Gurkha battalions under our command spread around the countryside and a massive signals squadron too. We would visit these regiments mostly by helicopter as in some locations this was the only way to get there. These guys also got their food and equipment by air drop.

It was a good job and I thoroughly enjoyed it. I settled in to being an RSM and realised the great deal of responsibility that I had, far more than I had really anticipated. I took drill, set the discipline and arranged duties as well as carrying out a certain amount of administration. I was responsible for health and safety and welfare. We did some rifle training and had some shooting matches against the battalions, those that were relieved because after a certain amount of time in a 'dirty' area you got brought back to rest and someone else replaced you. Back at HQ you could relax, recuperate and play sport. I made up a hockey team in Brigade HQ and we used to play the locals in Brunei. I also organised a boxing competition; the Gurkhas were not very good at boxing, but they enjoyed it. They were very good at handball games like basketball and my HQ combined with the signals squadron won the brigade basketball competition. We had a rifle section that did very well too. Here I must make it quite clear that I did not drill or train or in any way command the Gurkha troops, only those working in Brigade HQ. The Gurkha major and sergeant major looked after them and disciplinary matters were first tried by the Gurkha major.

This local role was a very good try-out for the job proper. I really enjoyed it and it enabled me to get to know exactly what would be expected of me in the rank (if I ever got it). I did get home on one week's R&R during that time.

We then got the message that we were moving. Things were getting better in Brunei; they had recovered all the land that had been occupied by the Indonesians and the state was now deemed free. We were told we were going to help top up all our battalions and moved down into Sarawak, which was a British state in Borneo at the time. We had to go down to Kuching, which was the capital of Sarawak because the Indonesians hadn't

*24. Off to Kuching*

been cleared out from over there as they had been in Brunei. There were still sporadic encounters with the invaders.

For the lads this was entirely different because it was a bigger, more widespread country and we now had battalions separated from Brigade HQ from up to a hundred miles away which we had to visit and re-supply. There was more jungle which meant that the soldiers had to learn to map-read and work their way through jungle terrain following tracks and things like that. It was so easy to get lost; they had to learn to set up ambushes and defensive areas.

We went back to Singapore and were there for three or four weeks, re-kitting and getting some more Gurkha recruits in as some people would be past their time and would be getting discharged. And off we sailed back over to Kuching. It was a nice place with quite a large number of ex-pats living and working there. So, despite the fact that we were still going out to monitor the units that we had all over the island, it was quite a pleasant HQ to be in.

Two remarkable things happened whilst I was in Borneo. The first was that now, under the command of my brigadier of 99 Brigade, came

1 Green Jackets, my old battalion who were now stationed in Penang Island just off Malaysia. They had been called in as well and put under command of 99 Brigade. Secondly, here I was, RSM of the Brigade HQ and on a par with me was the RSM of 1 Green Jackets, Derek Hornblower, one of my regimental mates whom I'd last seen in Kenya. I goaded him about seniority jokingly but he pooh-poohed it.

They had their HQ just outside of Kuching so I was able to go and visit them, socially more than anything else, because it was great to catch up with all my old mates in the sergeants' mess and a few of the officers.

The Commanding Officer of the battalion was Lieutenant Colonel David House, who later became a General and on retirement became 'Black Rod' in the House of Lords. He was in Brigade HQ one day and he happened to come and seek me out and told me that he wanted me back in the battalion.

'You've been away far too long, Sergeant Major,' he said. 'I want you back in the battalion because we are going to move back to Berlin when we've finished our tour here and I want you there with us.'

Now, although I was flattered by this I knew that Derek Hornblower was RSM at that time and I was mindful of my current acting rank. However when I mentioned this to the CO he said, 'Well, you won't be coming back as RSM. You're only local RSM here as you know.' He went on to explain that he wanted me back as CSM of A Company. 'We've had a bit of a problem with the current CSM,' and he went on to say that he was proving to be a bit of a liability and was going to be posted back to the UK. I said, 'I'm on Brigade HQ strength,' and he replied that I wasn't to worry as they weren't going yet but when they did go, he would be asking Brigade HQ to release me and post me back to the Battalion.

It actually turned out to be almost a year before that happened. But I did get a smashing annual report from the Brigadier, it was super.

CHAPTER 13

# CSM, Penang
# (1964–65)

I REJOINED THE BATTALION before they left Penang Island. Enid and the kids
were able to come with me and we spent three or four months there
before we came home. This gave us time to get back into the swing of the
regimental family again and me a chance to catch up with all my mates:
the likes of Joe Haydon, Doc Kempster and Derek Hornblower. It was
mostly entertainment and socialising – it was really great.

I discovered that during the time I'd been away my mate Punchy Morris
had left the army and was living in Cardiff where he had bought a sweet
shop. For me it was rather like a holiday really, with plenty of time off. We
explored the island and took the kids up to the top of Penang Hill on the
funicular railway.

*25. Penang Hill, funicular railway*

91

My Company Commander was Captain Julian Taylor who was going to take A Company to Berlin.

Not everyone was happy to be going to Berlin but they were about going home to England and having a few weeks off. It was going to be a completely different sort of soldiering in Berlin. We would be doing what we rudely referred to as 'bullshit' because we would always be in best kit and being shining examples; drill was important and saluting and everything else that had got rather casual when we were out in the jungle with our lives on the line!

The regiment came home early in 1965 and from here we all went to Berlin. As I was part of the advance party I didn't have a very long time back home. The advance party was responsible for getting the barracks ready for the troops. As a CSM I was responsible for our men's accommodation and barrack room allocation, getting information on duties such as night guards and making sure they could all settle in quickly when they got there. This was unusual, as these duties were normally the responsibility of the CQMSs but they were still in Penang to hand over to the incoming regiment who just happened to be 2 Green Jackets.

CHAPTER 14

# CSM – RQMS, Berlin
# (1965–66)

ALTHOUGH I DIDN'T HAVE A great deal of time back in England because I was part of the advance party, we did get a married quarter in Berlin almost immediately and so Enid and the family were able to come out rather quickly. In the Easter Bank Holiday I flew back to the UK to collect them. As I'd left my old car in Kenya we had brought a new one, a Ford Escort estate, and I drove it and the family back to Berlin. Being an estate we had a big boot and with the back seats let down, we put in a single mattress, which allowed the kids to have a lie-down when they were tired from the long journey.

We got a ferry from Dover to Zeebrugge in Belgium and then drove across Belgium to Germany. We stayed overnight in a B&B in Germany on the way. It was an interesting journey in itself as we had to drive through the 'eastern corridor' to get to West Berlin. We were monitored all the way; they gave you a time to set off and a time to arrive at your destination. Little planes kept flying over us checking to see if we were going at the correct speed and hadn't stopped at all. It was a bloody awful ride but nevertheless we arrived OK and this meant that for all the time we were in Berlin I had a car. Enid unfortunately, although she had attempted to drive whilst we were in Kenya, had not touched a car since and was unsure about her driving, particularly driving on the right, so she wasn't able to share the driving with me.

There was a British Military Children's School which Ian, and now Graham, attended – Graham's first school. Most of the other kids from our regiment went there too, so my two lads soon had many friends. Our regiment was located right at the intersection of the American zone and the East German border line. We were in a proper brick built barracks with company blocks, parade ground and sports fields and ironically right next to the Russian wire we had a pig farm which took care of the cookhouse 'swill' disposal. We were 17–20 miles from Berlin city centre.

We were in Berlin to be part of the four nation share-out of Berlin: British, American, French and Russian zones. We had to share duties that

93

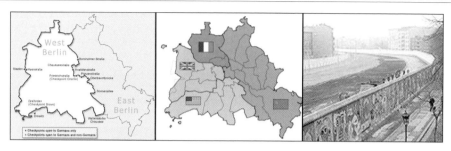

## A bit about the Berlin Wall

After the end of WWII in Europe, what remained of Nazi Germany west of the Oder-Neisse line was divided into four occupation zones (as per the Potsdam Agreement), each one controlled by one of the four occupying Allied powers: America, Britain, France and the Soviet Union. The capital, Berlin, was similarly subdivided into four sectors despite the city lying deep inside the Soviet zone. Within two years, relations between the Soviets and the other occupying powers had deteriorated. Stalin, the Soviet leader, planned a blockade which he believed would result in a united Germany under communist control. Hundreds of thousands of East Germans had already crossed into the West through Berlin and Stalin wanted to stop this. However the blockade failed and crossings continued. In 1952 the 'inner' German border was officially closed; a barbed wire fence was erected in 1961 and this was replaced by a permanent concrete wall in 1965. This remained in place for a quarter of a century until the border was reopened on 9 November 1989. During this time people still tried to cross to the West but this was now far more hazardous; around 200 people lost their lives attempting to escape; although over 5,000 were successful.

affected the German nationals rather than any particular country. It was a different kind of soldiering altogether from the Far East.

As I said, it was great to be back amongst my old mates; Derek Hornblower was still RSM of the battalion and Doc Kempster – one of my earliest buddies and one of my greatest competitors, shall we say, for seniority in the army – was the RQMS. As well as me there were Peter Bullen, Joe Haydon, Norman Bateman and Johnny Trahearn who were all strong CSMs. We had a great sergeants' mess and anyone in the army will tell you if you have a good sergeants' mess you have a good battalion. John Stevenson was QM; we had all served under him when he was RSM. John left on retirement during our tour and was replaced by Don Truluck, whom I had served with at Sandhurst.

26. *Enid and the kids at the regimental sports day, Don and Mrs Truluck enjoying the joke*

Our married quarter was a lovely three-bedroom apartment in a block of flats. On the same landing as us were Derek Hornblower and his wife Beryl – she was a good friend of Enid's – and their two kids Stephen and Yvonne. There was talk of him getting a commission very shortly, so remembering what the CO had said, I was keeping my fingers crossed.

Berlin was, in some ways, like being on an island but instead of being surrounded by water you were encircled by hostile land and hemmed in by barbed wire. The whole purpose of us being there was it seemed political rather than military, flying the flag and visibly showing one's muscles. As part of the Berlin Brigade we had to share responsibilities with two other infantry battalions, namely the Somerset and Cornwall Light Infantry (SCLI) and 3 Royal Anglian Regiment; at the end of 1965 the SCLI were replaced by 1st Royal Inniskilling Fusiliers.

Brigade duty battalion came in four month rotations. During that time you supplied men as sentries for Brigade HQ, the Russian war memorial at Tiergaten, armed escort on the daily train to West Germany through the East German 'corridor' to Brunswick plus the 'big one' guarding Spandau

Prison. We took over from the French with a special hand-over ceremony and handed over to the Russians.

As the regiment had arrived around Easter we had missed the January rotation but as we picked up our duties in May, my Company, 'A' Company, were assigned the Spandau duty. There were six towers around the prison that needed to be manned: four soldiers in each at any one time. This duty was not shared out like many others. Most of the lads and indeed I myself got to see Rudolf Hess doing his exercises in the grounds of the prison. That was rather special.

The only two prisoners left in Spandau Prison when we took over were Hess and Albert Speer. Speer was released owing to poor health (he had served almost all of his twenty years sentence) later in 1966, so when Hess committed suicide in 1987 Spandau Prison was left empty. In order to ensure that the prison didn't become a memorial to Neo-Nazis the German authorities tore it down and dumped the rubble in the North Sea.

On the lighter side in 1966 England beat West Germany in the final of the World Cup and of course great joy was felt by our regiment and the British people who were serving in Berlin at the time. I'm afraid we did take the mickey a bit by driving around with Union Jacks flying when we heard the result.

A funny incident occurred a few days after the match, at the petrol station where I always went to fill up my car. I was on good terms with the petrol attendant there and he asked me, 'Why are you flying that flag?' and I replied, 'Because we beat your lot at football.' He then said, 'Well, I am not giving you any petrol; you will have to go elsewhere. I don't like people making fun of us.' Of course he was only joking but it was interesting to see that they were feeling a little bit down in the mouth and it was true that some of our people were taking it a bit too far. They drove around with banners on their cars that said things like, 'Can you Germans win at anything? We beat you in the war and we've beaten you at football now,' and things like that. I think it was a bit too much but that's how it was, for a short time.

During the time we were in Berlin many sporting events took place, particularly football, with the Berlin Brigade league major units, of which there were quite a few apart from the three British battalions. There were Royal Signals there, REME, a very big ordnance depot and an RAF station up at Gatow, so there was a hell of a lot of troops there, all coming under Berlin Brigade. Derek Hornblower and I became the football officers for

Note from author:

Unfortunately I missed the final having left the battalion on promotion to RSM

## FOOTBALL

After our successes in the Penang F.A. leagues the Battalion football team approached its first season in European type football for some years with, if nothing else, a great deal of confidence. The same players who had achieved our previous successes were still available, and the cry was, what we had done before we can do again.

Having only played local sides in Penang we were not too sure that we could achieve the same amount of success against major unit sides of equal strength.

However, directly after the Royal Review was over, nightly training sessions were held both in the Gymnasium and on the numerous Soccer pitches in barracks. These were run by R.Q.M.S. Lawless who as many older readers will remember, was a Battalion player of considerable ability in days gone by. These training sessions were culminated with a series of trial games, and an XI was picked to represent the Battalion against 3rd Battalion Royal Anglian Regiment in a friendly. The result was, the Battalion 8, 3rd Battalion Royal Anglian Regiment 1. This boosted our confidence, and the next match against a strong R.A.F. Gatow side resulted in a draw 3.3.

The Battalion then entered the Berlin Infantry Major Units League, the Berlin Infantry Brigade Knock Out competition and the Army Cup.

The Battalion finished second in the Major Units League, on goal average, to 1st Battalion Somerset and Cornwall Light Infantry having only lost one game.

A short mention of the two games against 1 S.C.L.I. is worth recording. Our first game away we beat them 7.4, and in the return on our own ground we lost 4.2.

In the Army Cup our success was short lived. In the first round we beat 18 Field Regiment R.A. 2.1 in what was the best game of the season. But in the next round we were beaten 3.0 by the Black Watch at Minden. The result however might have been very different if we had not scored an own goal and missed a penalty!

The latter part of the season was taken up playing the Major Units Knock Out which the Battalion won easily only conceding one goal. The final was played on the Brigade ground against Alexander Barracks, the score being 6.0.

the battalion and I used to train them and get them out in the evenings on the playing fields and also work with them back in the gym. This had never happened before; usually they just picked a team and off they'd go. But we had such fantastic facilities in Berlin that I was able to get together a group of thirty or so good class lads who were vying for places in the battalion team. I got them working and working hard and it did pay off because we won the Berlin Brigade league, major units and also they did very well against local teams, some of which were really quite good.

We stayed in Berlin for nearly two years during which time quite a few things happened. Changes in promotion took place. Six months after we arrived in Berlin Doc Kempster was promoted to RSM and went to the Rifle Depot back in the UK, and I got promoted to replace him as RQMS.

Later in the year Derek Hornblower was commissioned and after a short course in the UK came back as Lt. (QM) MTO (Motor Transport Officer) in about August of 1966; this left a vacancy for RSM. They did not promote me because Doc Kempster had already been earmarked for it. So after his short 'holiday' at the Rifle Depot, Doc Kempster returned to the Battalion to take over RSM from Derek Hornblower.

So for a short period of time I was RQMS whilst Doc Kempster was RSM. As two senior warrant officers we had our preferred ways of doing things and we didn't always see eye to eye. Remember I had taken over the role of RQMS from Doc Kempster and he had his way of doing accounting and I had mine and we had some differences of opinion on that: nothing to go to higher authorities on, rather something that we had to sort out between ourselves which we did.

Around this time I found out that I was the next person qualified for WO1 substantively, presumably through the period of time in my current rank and the experience I had (the period with the Gurkhas was now paying off). Clearly the regiment didn't want to lose me because they said they would find me a job – and they did.

It just happened that the current Rifle Depot RSM, who had taken over from Doc Kempster when he was recalled to the Battalion – the 'holiday' that I alluded to earlier – only had a few months left to do. I was earmarked for that job and I was briefed by the CO who informed me of this but said that in the interim the regiment would find me a temporary post. I was promoted officially to WO1 from that date and my pay, status and authority was now assured in that rank. I was pleased that before I left for the UK the CO invited me to lunch with all the officers in the officers' mess.

Berlin was a great place. Gladys, Enid's mother, came out to visit us for a holiday and stayed for ten weeks! But all good things have to come to an end and I left Berlin. I decided to leave our car there and I gave it away to one of the Signal Platoon boys who had just got his family out there. It wasn't going to last very much longer anyway.

# CHAPTER 15

# RSM, Bristol University OTC
# (1966–67)

THE JOB THE REGIMENT FOUND ME was a temporary posting, to Bristol University as RSM of the Officer Training Corps (OTC).

I left Berlin on 7 September and had about ten days' leave before I took Enid and the kids to Bristol. Whilst we were on leave I bought a new (to me) car, and that's how we travelled there. Through a minor error in map reading, our first entry into the city was via the impressive Clifton suspension bridge, designed by Brunel.

On arrival at the university building, I met everyone involved in the organisational set-up there: the CO; one of the 'beaks' at the university; and also the 2IC, a regular army major from the Gloucestershire Regiment.

*27. Divisional Brigadier and Commanding Officer of the OTC presenting me with my Long Service and Good Conduct Medal in the Drill Hall at Bristol University, April 1967*

After a thorough briefing and obtaining directions on how to find our quarter Enid gathered up the kids, who had been playing football with a PT instructor in the gym, and we set off to find our new home. Our married quarter was in Westbury-on-Trymm on the outskirts of the city.

The OTC had NCO weapon training instructors, so my role as the RSM was just a supervisory one. I was responsible for the stores and equipment, and gave the odd lecture, and a few talks, to pass on the benefits of my experience. I also supervised all the shooting and range work on the nearby rifle ranges.

Two events of some significance happened during my time at Bristol. First, in April 1967 I was presented with my long service and good conduct medal (LS and GC) by the area brigadier. This medal is awarded for eighteen years continuous service and an unblemished record.

Secondly, on 25 July I was called to Winchester for the Queen's Review of the regiment. Following on from the grand parade and march past, Her Majesty The Colonel in Chief graciously sat for a photograph with all the warrant officers and sergeants who had been on parade that day, plus all other warrant officers and senior NCOs of her newly titled regiment who, like myself, were stationed elsewhere.

It was a day to remember!!

Back in Bristol on the social side I met up with another old mate that I had previously served with, ex WO2 Ken Young and his wife Mary. Ken was now retired from the army and was working for the city council. Enid and I spent many happy hours with them. Enid's mother, Gladys, came and stayed with us for a couple of weeks, whilst the boys were on holiday from school.

Nothing more than humdrum activities took place, until one day in December, I got a telephone call from the adjutant of the Rifle Depot to ask how immersed in Bristol I was and would there be a problem with a quick move. I said no because all my books and accounts were up to date and there was nothing to keep me there. The move was so quick that I hadn't time to arrange for a furniture removal van or anything. Winchester sent down a 4-ton truck for all our stuff and dropped it at the married quarter to await our arrival. This meant that before I reported to the barracks, Enid and I were able to unload and partly sort out all our belongings – a rare thing on arriving at a new posting. I then said, 'Ta-ra then, love, see you when I see you,' and walked straight into the depot.

28. *The Royal Review. Her Majesty the Queen, Colonel-in-Chief, at the Warrant Officers' and Sergeants' Mess, by the Lower Pavillion, St Cross*

# CHAPTER 16

# RSM, Rifle Depot, Winchester (1967–69)

UNUSUALLY, WHEN I ARRIVED at the depot I did not have anyone to take over from, as the recent incumbent RSM Bill Williams had already left. This was why there was so much urgency in getting me there. Bill had been commissioned and had been posted to Hong Kong, I think, to join the Gurkhas as quartermaster. Normally you would have a hand-over period with your predecessor where you would be briefed on operational and personal issues and eased into the role. Although I didn't get this it didn't really matter because I had been an RSM before and I knew what was expected. I just picked up from where my predecessor had left off and gradually brought in my own changes as time went on.

Now I was definitely and surely an RSM, not only an RSM but RSM of the regimental depot and slowly becoming a key figure in regimental affairs. For example I was working with the Old Comrades Associations, who used the sergeants' mess for their monthly meetings. I was also instrumental in forming – together with the RSM of the Light Infantry depot in Shrewsbury – the new drill to be adopted by the whole division. I had two weeks in Copthorne Barracks, Shrewsbury, and then he came to our depot in Winchester for another two weeks. The two respective adjutants made the final assessment and agreed to the new form of drill, which I think is still being used as I write this.

We put Ian into Montgomery of Alamein Boarding School and whilst he was there the school did the musical *Oliver*, and Ian played the lead role of Oliver. This was a highlight for the family with Enid getting involved too; she was part of a crowd scene where people were selling things in the street.

We had a good sergeants' mess and all NCOs were supportive of me.

In my time we had four passing out parades. I played the early part in the passing out parades prior to the troops marching on. I'd make a speech to all the parents and visitors, welcoming them there and telling everyone

29. *Monthly Passing Out Parade. RSM Lawless, Major J. Mason, CSM Taylor,
Lieut.-Colonel D.M. Stileman, Captain A.E. Berry, Lieutenant J.D. Stephens,
Major-General P.G.F. Young, Cpl Hill, Sgt George*

all that the lads had achieved during their training – in truth it was much
the same speech from parade to parade. I'd announce who was Inspecting
Officer of the day and then march back to the edge of the parade ground
and welcome the inspection party, whether it was a General or whoever it
might be, and fall in with them to inspect the troops. In proper military
fashion I would move slightly ahead of the inspection party, winking at the
young rifleman, trying to get them to relax and telling them to stand still,
be smart and give a good impression and generally encouraging them to
show off.

One of my duties was, occasionally, to give the young officers sword drill
at 7 o'clock in the morning behind the gymnasium so that the young
recruits couldn't see them being drilled.

I was also responsible for the running of the sergeants' mess and the well
being of all the people in it. I had to detail the barrack duties: the orderly
sergeant and the night guard, and check that working parties were all
properly organised and dressed correctly. Not that I actually picked
anybody for working parties. I would just tell the sergeant majors how

104

many NCOs and men were required, and when and where, and they did the rest. Supervision of the regimental police, the guardroom, cells and prisoners were all under my jurisdiction and also occasionally, checking and inspecting defaulters, commonly called 'Janker Wallahs'.

It was a very good job even though it was rather different from my previous RSM experience with the Gurkhas because these were a different sort of soldier. I was supervising the training of recruits now and not experienced men; however the principles were the same.

The sergeants' mess had a wonderful event each year called the Peninsula Ball – Peninsula being the title of a regimental battle honour. The previous year's ball had been a great success and everyone was still talking about it. So I, being me, set my sights on making this one even better. Which indeed was the case, even if I say so myself.

We had a big married quarter with four bedrooms, so we were able to invite people to stay with us overnight. RSM Johnny Trahearn and his wife Nancy came to stay with us; John was the RSM of the Territorial Battalion in Oxford at the time. My mother and stepfather also came down from Yorkshire to attend the ball, as well as Enid's mother Gladys. We all certainly had a ball!

The time I had at Winchester was marvellous. On the sporting front I started off a hockey team. We were allowed to practise on the drill square which under normal circumstances no one was allowed casually to walk on. We had a proper hockey pitch, established away from the camp, where we used to play all our matches.

Also on the social side the Colonel Commandant of the Light division (Lt. General Sir Anthony Read, KCB, CBE, DSO, MC) on a visit to the depot came into the sergeants' mess to talk to all the members, followed by a photograph. The pertinent part of his speech was to emphasise the need of both regiments, Light Infantry and Royal Green Jackets, to work together and mingle and become one big happy family so that the Light Division as a whole would benefit.

In view of his remarks I contacted the RSM of 1LI (1st Light Infantry) who were stationed in Gravesend, Kent and arranged with him to get the two sergeants' messes together for a weekend. The 1LI RSM, Robert (Bob) Cox –whom I will mention more later on in this chapter – lost the toss, so the 1LI had to entertain us. I took all of our mess to Gravesend, less those on depot duties. We travelled on Saturday by coach arriving late morning. We had previously arranged the itinerary and after lunch (a wet

30. Sergeants' mess, The Rifle Depot, May 1968. Back row – Sgts Lacey, Bayliss, B. Maj Chapman, Sgts Bristow, Read, McClusky, Smith, S. Sgt Perrin. Centre row – C. Sgt Wigger, Sgt Howard, Sgt McNamara, C. Sgt Jones, S. Sgts Kirby, Williams, Wood, Sgts Sanders, Evans, Fisher, Jukes, C. Sgt Thompson MM. Front row – WOII Smith, RQMS Dunwell, Cpt Berry, Lt Gen Read, Lt Col Jackson, WOIIs Parker-Smith, Skinner, Taylor, Sykes, RSM Lawless, WOIs Pinkney, Williams, WOII Baird

one I might add) we played a football match. We lost marginally – I can't remember the score – but we should have had at least three penalties. The referee was blatantly biased!

After a further super evening meal, we engaged in indoor games: darts, crib, dominos, and so on, and we finally won on the 'sink a pint' play-off. Very late, we all retired, some into a spare barrack room, most in the mess. The RSM and his good lady had invited me to stay in a spare room in their married quarter – rank sometimes does have its privileges. We all attended a church service next morning and after lunch departed for Winchester. I'm sure that many new friends were made over that weekend.

Bob Cox, later in his career, was commissioned and served with the Gurkhas. He finally retired as a Lieutenant Colonel. In later years, because of golf, I found out that our lives had been very similar. He had been born and brought up in the same South Yorkshire district as me. Although he was two years younger than me he had taken the same route through the army as I had: National Service at Bordon, Lance Corporal after training, Light Infantry albeit the Somerset Light Infantry, and going on to become a regular. All this I found out when he was captaining the Hampshire Past Captains Golf Society and I was captaining the Society of London Golf Captains. Now I am getting ahead of myself!

All in all I enjoyed being the RSM of the depot. Although I had some wonderful times in my military career, as far as I'm concerned, my time here was the most rewarding to me, not just for the promotion opportunities that this might lead to but because I loved the job and the people I worked with. I hope that everyone felt that I carried out my duties to the very highest standards. My proudest moments were seeing these youngsters come in off the streets and end up the finished article. This was mainly due to the high standard of the NCO instructors; in particular four young corporals impressed me with their diligence, enthusiasm and subject knowledge. I am proud to say that these Corporals: Roy Stanger, Mick Gleeson, Bob Fortune and Micky Hill, were all later in their careers given commissions.

I still thought that when I left the depot I would get a commission to quartermaster just like my mate Derek Hornblower. Doc Kempster didn't get it because he wanted to go out having done his 22 years, so that put me in the frame for quartermaster. Joe Hayden hadn't got to RSM – he was certainly good enough – because he had decided to take voluntary redundancy whilst still a CSM. These guys were my counterparts, people who I joined up with; they were the same age and had similar promotional ambitions and opportunities. All the way through our careers we'd been battling with each other and always these two had been slightly ahead of me. Joe and I became CQMSs together, Doc Kempster got to become a CSM, then RQMS and RSM before me. Joe was a CSM before I was. We followed each other's careers and as far as I was concerned these two were my main competitors; but we were good mates too. We used to pull each other's legs all the time and say things like, 'How the bloody hell did you get sergeant major before me?' and other unmentionable comments.

So you can imagine how surprised I was when the CO called me into his office and told me that it looked as if I wasn't going to get a quartermaster's position. He explained that now we were in the Light Division we were allowed to promote three quartermasters from the ranks each year. Although I now came into that bracket there were only three to a division and these were split between the Light Infantry and the Green Jackets. This was done by allocating two to one regiment and one to the other, then swapping the allocations around the next year. Unfortunately this year we only got one position and he told me the bloke's name that had already been given it. I couldn't really complain because this bloke was senior to me (even if I personally thought I might have been the better choice, but then, I would, wouldn't I?). He told me I'd have to wait until next year but what to do with me in the meantime? I couldn't stay at the depot because I'd be holding up somebody else's promotion. He told me he'd found me a job that would continue with a merit element, commanding 46 Army Youth Team down at Woolwich. The CO said we'd have to wait and see how we went on from there. I asked whether this would be a stepping-stone to a commission and he confirmed that it could be. He said he knew I'd like to get one now, but we had to stick to our allocations. Next year we would have two places.

However that didn't help me!

CHAPTER 17

# RSM, 46 Army Youth Team, Woolwich (1969–70)

So I WENT OFF TO WOOLWICH.

We left Ian in boarding school in Winchester. He was happy to stay; all the kids called him Oliver and he had made many friends there. We had been allocated a nice married quarter, and quite near the Barracks too, so convenient. Graham's school wasn't far away either.

Having introduced myself to my predecessor – a lieutenant whose name I'm afraid I can't remember – we had a week together handing/taking over and then he left.

Within a week I was called back to see the Regimental Colonel. He said, 'I'm sorry to have to tell you that you are going to miss out on becoming a quartermaster. Now I don't want you to get upset. Records have said that you would be entitled, with the proper recommendation and we would provide that, to a short service commission as a lieutenant in one of three places: Ordnance Corp, Royal Signals or Royal Engineers. I'd suggest the Ordnance Corp as that would fit in with your experience.'

Well, I didn't want to leave the regiment and I told him so. I said, 'I have been in this regiment, in one form or another, for twenty-odd years and it is my life.'

'Well,' he said, 'it would be temporary. You would still be in consideration to come back as a quartermaster.'

I said, 'But you can't give me any guarantees on that, can you, Sir?'

'Well,' he replied, 'I can't do anything else for you at the moment. I've talked to Records and they say everything must be done by the book.'

I thanked him for seeing me and mentioned that I wanted to stay in the army and that being commissioned would have ensured that, so the short service commission was probably the only solution. He then told me, which I knew anyway, that I could probably only stay in until I was fifty-five (I was approaching forty at the time) as this was the usual age limit for anybody. He added, 'I'm sorry but don't give up hope. We'll still keep trying.'

And that was the end of that, but I have to say I was gutted.

I talked to Enid about the situation and explained that I was being offered a lieutenant's position. I'd be at the beck and call of everyone and I wouldn't even be in my own regiment. As normal, she understood how I felt and said that she would be happy with whatever I decided. So I told the Regimental Colonel that I didn't want the short service commission and if push came to shove I would leave the army. To his credit he accepted that. He congratulated me on my efforts at the depot and told me to stay at my current position with the youth team for the time being.

So far, I haven't said very much about our work with 46. We were essentially trying to give a good impression to teenagers about life in the army and showing off our skills, be they soldierly or otherwise. We had specially selected soldiers in the team with varying skills. One was a qualified projectionist, two other lads were Bisley standard riflemen – particularly useful when teaching youngsters small bore shooting on the 25-yard range, another was a lance corporal who was a wizard with a football; he could entertain any audience, not just kids, with his tricks. All the team had a part to play. The composition of the team was: the commander, usually an officer; a sergeant; and ten others, two of whom were drivers. Because we were trying to sell the army to the public, the younger element in particular, we always, whatever function we were performing, had to be in the correct uniform and always smartly dressed. We visited youth organisations, public schools and colleges, YMCAs etc. Nearly all of these visits were by appointment and in the evening. Our daily routine was to attend a muster parade at 08:30 each day; this was necessary because whilst most of the team lived in the artillery barracks, some lived in married quarters and in my team, one lad lived with his parents in Woolwich with my permission. After muster parade we would retire to our office and sort out arrangements for our evening visits and gather together all the equipment we needed. The drivers would carry out the usual POL (petrol, oil and lubricants) inspection and then at about 12:30 we would all fall out until the appointed time in the evening.

My sergeant was a golfer and he had often asked me to have a try at the game. I'd resisted, saying I couldn't see any fun in hitting a little white ball and chasing after it. He wasn't put off and told me that there was a 9-hole pitch and putt course in Danson Park near Bexley just down the road from Woolwich. He said, 'Come and have a bash at that and see how you get on.'

By now Enid had got a part time job. Ian was away at boarding school and Graham was at the local school, therefore in the afternoons I was often at a loose end, so one afternoon I succumbed and went with my sergeant to play 9 holes of golf. I did this on a few occasions after that and I really got the bug, discovering that I could hit the ball. We gradually moved on to other public courses; we played the one at Hainault for a while and went as far afield as Whitewebbs in Crews Hill, Enfield and Epping Forest where we had to wear red clothing.

I had got friendly with the gunners' chief clerk. He was a warrant officer and we would often have a drink together. On one occasion I was bemoaning my military fate. I said, 'What is the point of being in the bloody army now?' I was telling him about my ambitions and how I'd missed out on becoming a QM and that my 22 years engagement was up and any time now they would be giving me my cards and there was nothing I could do about it.

To my surprise he replied, 'Yes, there is. If you are intent on staying in the army why don't you apply to go on the Long Service List [LSL]? Then you can stay in until you are fifty-five. You won't get any more promotion but you'll keep your present rank.'

Well I knew nothing about the LSL and asked him if he could let me have the full details. This he did and after a bit of research I found out that the most important job on the LSL seemed to be in recruiting – the army were looking at this as being one of their biggest assets – crucial to keep the army up to strength. I asked the Chief Clerk whom I should speak to about this and he told me that I would have to apply to my own regiment to be put on the LSL.

'Oh bloody hell; this is a step down, isn't it?' I sighed.

'Certainly not,' he replied, 'you get to keep your rank, don't you?'

I said, 'Yes, but there are no commissioned jobs, are there?'

'No,' he replied, 'but you do get to stay in until you're fifty-five.'

Well I wasn't exactly happy about this but I went home to talk to Enid about this development. We sat down and had a long chat and examined all the options. I said, 'Look, luv, I want to stay in the army because the army is my life. If I came out, what would I do? I'm a trained killer; what sort of job does that get me in Civvi Street? If I do this then I can go on until I'm fifty-five. Which is better than forty-two.'

I was obviously thinking about my pension and how Enid and I would live once I did leave the army. Typical of Enid, she said, 'If that is what you want, then stay in.'

The next day I telephoned Winchester and arranged an interview with the Regimental Colonel – the one who had basically told me that I had no future in the army. I went to the depot and told him that I had found myself a job. He asked me what I meant and I explained that I'd been asking around and found out that I qualified for the Long Service List.

'I'd forgotten all about that,' he said, 'is that what you want to do?'

'Yes,' I said. 'Can I do it and stay in the regiment?'

He replied, 'Yes, but not in a battalion. You'd have to be on ERE [Extra Regimental Employment]. Leave it with me and I'll get the chief clerk to arrange it for you. He'll contact you with all the arrangements as soon as possible.' And I went home.

Well, I don't know what he did but I got a call from the chief clerk within days to tell me that he had all the paperwork ready for me to sign. Could I call into his office because the regimental colonel wanted me to get to Winchester on Friday morning – today was Wednesday? I was planned for a Boy's Club display on Friday so I handed the job to my sergeant, the first time I had delegated any job to him.

Off I went to see the Colonel. He said, 'You are going to be the senior recruiter in the Central London Recruiting Depot [CLRD] on the strength of Headquarters London District. You will keep your rank and pay and you will work under Major McDermott who's the Officer IC Recruiting London District. It's a good job and you will do well in it. And what's more you'll be a Green Jacket and that, from our point of view, is a good thing too.'

I thanked him and went to sign my forms with the chief clerk. I was also given an interview time and date to go and see Major Mac, as he was usually referred to.

When I met with Major Mac he also introduced me to my predecessor, WO1 Green, an RCM (Regimental Corporal Major) of the cavalry, who was retiring from the army. Major Mac, who was also retiring shortly, asked me what I wanted out of the job. 'Well firstly, I want to do a good job,' I said, 'and I'm sure that you will ensure that I do. But mainly I want to stay in the army until I'm fifty-five.' I explained that I wanted to do the whole whack as this would enhance my pension and terminal grant and considerably help with my finances when I eventually left the army. He asked me about married quarters and was I going to stay in Woolwich? I told him I would prefer to move nearer to central London. He asked me, 'What's nearer to Central London than Woolwich?' However he went on to say that there were some new married quarters being built in Whetstone in North London. I asked about public transport: tubes and buses, for getting into work and he told me that Whetstone was at the end of the Northern Line so I wouldn't have any problems getting a seat.

He also asked how many bedrooms I would need in the quarter.

'We could manage with two but three would be better,' I answered.

'Right,' he said. 'I'll get on to the married families' officer and ask him if you can have a three-bedroomed quarter in Sweets Way, Whetstone.'

There was a three-bedroomed married quarter available and it was assigned to me for the duration.

I handed over my Army Youth Team to an officer, having taken over from an officer, sorted out my married quarter in Woolwich and reported for duty to CLRD which was on New Scotland Yard just off Whitehall.

# CHAPTER 18

# WOI, Central London Recruiting Depot
# (1970–75)

WITHIN A WEEK OF STARTING AT the Central London Recruiting Depot (CLRD) I was back in Woolwich attending a recruiting course at the Army School of Recruiting. I didn't commute home but stayed in the gunners' sergeants' mess throughout the week and went home at weekends. The course lasted for four weeks. As well as meeting up again with most of the mess members, there was another WO1 on the course – Chick Douglas of the Scots Guards who had been at Sandhurst with me and had been a CSM there. I enjoyed the course and learned a lot about recruiting. I also went to Bicester in Oxfordshire to do a projectionist course, which I duly passed. This was so I could show films to potential recruits. All this happened in the first couple of months.

On the family front Ian had been a boarder at Winchester and was now of school leaving age. He didn't want to stay at school so we got him a job with Ridgeway's Tea Company. He was sixteen years old. We put Graham into Queen Elizabeth Boy's School in Barnet. Enid's mother came and stayed with us for a few weeks helping us settle in and that was fine. She had the spare bedroom, and after that it was always her room whenever she came to stay.

The sergeants' mess in CRLD was in the same building as the recruiting office, so we didn't have to go very far to the sergeants' mess. Ironically the garrison sergeant major, who controlled the sergeants' mess, was RSM Tom Taylor – we had been bumping into each other since 1948. Remember, Tom was a platoon sergeant at the Guards' junior NCO training battalion at Sennelager with me and then we met again at Sandhurst where he was a sergeant major to my colour sergeant. Now here he was again in London District as the senior person in the sergeants' mess. During the next few years I got to know Tom very well – he was a great guy. He carried on in his garrison sergeant major's job for a heck of a long time. There was a great deal of ceremonial duties and he did these tremendously well.

31. *Army School of Recruiting – Recruiters' Course in Advanced Studies (me, front row, centre) February 1972*

As a Warrant Officer 1 (WO1) as well, I used to help out when I could in Tom's sergeants' mess. I volunteered for our recruiters to be the social committee. We had a few functions including one night when we laid on a sort of Lonnie Donegan skiffle evening. It went very well and everybody came in – the wives too, from various places – to dance to our skiffle group. The group's instruments were made up of a tea chest with a broom handle coming out of it and a piece of string strung tight between it and a frying pan with holes drilled in it and some cat wire strung across it. We also had a very talented lad with a squeezebox – one of these accordion things – and it all went very well. Tom Taylor approved what we were doing for the mess and it was always busy.

In the same building as CRLD were the district cells and we had a lot of senior NCOs and cell duty people coming and going. The cells were really a halfway stage for deserters or recalcitrant soldiers who had been picked up and brought back to London, who were held in the cells waiting to be taken back to their various regiments to be dealt with.

One of the more pleasant duties I had whilst at CLRD was to volunteer to be a senior services steward at Wimbledon; I did this for four years in succession. The services, as they still do today, provided all the stewards on all courts during the Wimbledon fortnight. As Senior Warrant Officer, I was mainly on centre court and when royalty were in the Royal Box I would be on duty there. No doubt many viewers would have seen me on TV – we were asked to keep a low profile but you sometimes got caught on camera. This role was voluntary and you gave up two weeks of your annual leave to do it. The tennis association paid you and very good pay it was too. As senior steward I collected all the pay packets and distributed them to the others. I was also responsible for the allocation of stewards to courts, gangways and stairs.

I was finding that the workload at CLRD was easing, the longer it went on. I made more visits to the outstations, sometimes just to get out of the office, where I would be sat twiddling my thumbs. Visits, of course, were necessary for the collection of reports which all had to be logged in central records. It was important for us to know how many candidates were in the pipeline and at what stage they were: i.e. how many had passed the Matrix Test, how many had passed medicals, how many were waiting for medicals, how many had been accepted by the unit of their choice and so on and so forth. We were constantly being asked for numbers by higher authorities.

During the time I was at CLRD three sergeant recruiters and a CSM from my regiment were on our staff. It was obvious to me that our

*32. Army Golf Club 1976. Best 1–12 Score*

regiment were serious about recruiting. For most other regiments recruiters were usually older, as if they had reached their sell-by dates and were just seeing out their time, whilst ours were younger, more keen and eager to do well, for the sake of their careers.

My interest in golf continued. With a bit more time on my hands I was now able to play more often so I joined the London District Golf Society or, more precisely, helped to start a society, together with Captain Campbell (Peanuts) Graham who was District Officer for Physical Training (DOPT) in District Headquarters. The society was a success and became very popular. We had a golf meeting once a month at the Army Golf Club in Aldershot, which was always well attended. I continued to attend meetings for the next fifteen or so years. I can't leave this subject without saying that I did win one or two trophies over this time.

After the second year in CLRD I had a bit more time on my hands owing to being on top of the job. Enid and I were able to take regular holidays together and we went to Dubrovnik, Yugoslavia for two weeks on a fairly regularly basis. In fact we went five times in the next eight years; each time for a fortnight and to the same hotel, the Villa Dubrovnik.

*33. Villa Dubrovnik*

Before we went the first time Enid couldn't swim. Dubrovnick is on the Adriatic Sea and the water was so warm and salty that you could virtually float, so this seemed a good time for her to learn but she just couldn't force herself to lift her feet off the bottom. However there was a life jacket at the steps into the sea and I coaxed her into wearing this to give her more confidence. Well, the first time she tried this, it was hilarious. Off she shoved into the deep and lo and behold, she turned completely upside down – she had put it on the wrong way up! I helped her to righten herself but I couldn't stop laughing. I rather stupidly said, 'I thought it was a whale.' Well, she gave me such a clout with the life jacket saying, 'You can stuff your swimming.' She did persevere however and eventually learnt to swim. But the sight of Enid up-ended in the water will stay with me always.

Another thing about the hotel was that they had quite a few different souvenirs including T-shirts but as with everything in the hotel they had printed on them the hotel's logo, which was entwined letters V and D. We took one home the first year as a present for our son Graham. When he saw it he said, 'If you think I'm walking down the high street with that on, you can think again!'

It was about this time that I decided that I wanted to join a proper golf club so with the help of my old mate Derek Hornblower, who was now the Quartermaster with the 4th Battalion in Davies Street, Mayfair, I joined Richmond Park Golf Club as part of a society; we were about forty strong. As Richmond Park was a public course and our society had few privileges, you had to book and pay each time you played. Our medal rounds were always on Sundays which meant that every four weeks eight or nine of us would have to be at the golf club very early so that we could book our 4-ball matches. To some it entailed sleeping in the car all night – I was one of these. I got my first official handicap there – it was 18. A year later I got it down to 14.

Then it hit me. I was being rather stupid. I was a society member at Richmond Park but in Whetstone, about a quarter of a mile down the road from Sweets Way, where I lived, was a private club called North Middlesex Golf Club. Here was I every fourth week watching match of the day on Saturday night, then leaving to drive to Richmond Park and roughing it in my car overnight to book a game of golf for other people. I decided that I would try to join North Middlesex. In 1972 I put in a written application to join and I was eventually accepted with a confirmed handicap of 14. I was pleasantly surprised to find that the Secretary was no other than Captain (retd) Bob Merry late of the Small Arms School Corps (SASC) who had been a sergeant major instructor when I did my course at Hythe in 1952, and later together we met up again when my regiment was up from Berlin, in Sennelager doing their fortnight's annual training. We quickly retired to the bar.

From then on I was playing golf almost every weekend and sometimes in the week too if my schedule allowed it. I asked Derek Hornblower to come to North Mid as my guest on a number of occasions and sometimes on a Sunday he would bring his wife Beryl and their two kids and they would stay with Enid whilst Derek and I played golf. Afterwards we would all sit down to a roast lunch. Enid and I became regular visitors to the golf club and we did get involved with the social activities – more on that a bit later.

Whilst in CLRD I have to say that I was more or less looked upon as being the 'spy in the camp'. I was a Green Jacket, remember, amongst a predominant number of Guardsmen who had a heavy influence on what was going on in London District, so I was able to give information back to my regiment about the way things were done on such and such a day or how they went about doing a particular parade, e.g. in slow time – all sorts of snippets of information that I would pass back to the regiment or would tell somebody if they asked me.

As we were recruiting I had a wide geographical area, reaching into Essex, Middlesex (where I had an office in Finchley) and various places north of the river (I had offices in places like Forest Green and Blackheath). We did have a very big area to cover and this kept me busy, moving from office to office making sure that everything was going well and helping out where I could. Bear in mind that a lot of our offices also recruited for the navy and the RAF – these were more general recruiting offices but they all came under my jurisdiction. So I got to know London pretty well which apart from other advantages made me very useful when friends and family came down from Yorkshire to visit London because I knew where I was going and could take them out and show them the sights!

We did on odd occasions have to carry out certain duties within Headquarters London District itself, particularly in the old building. I remember that one or two of our recruiters were asked to help out in the general canteen – it wasn't really a mess because there were more civilian than military staff working in the HQ – which we did along with other departments.

We also helped out with the Trooping of the Colour; as working parties in some cases where we were setting out chairs and things like that, escorting people to seats and so on. We were also in a position to obtain tickets for seats normally reserved for the press (basic hard seats not the posh cushioned ones for dignitaries) at the actual parade, not just for the rehearsal. I was able to invite some of my friends from the golf club and some of my ex-army mates from the Old Comrades Association.

Generally speaking recruiting was not an irksome job; in fact it was quite satisfying sometimes. I must have had a score of young lads come back to see me at CRLD, after they'd been in for eighteen months or two years, and were passing through London. They would call in to say, Thanks, Sir, for getting us into the army and everything you've done for us.' That was really rewarding.

We did assist the Army Youth Teams which were predominant around the London area. I knew exactly what they did from my time commanding 46 Army Youth Team. We helped out in their cases with recruiting, promotional materials and photographic equipment and in some cases our recruiters would accompany the teams if they were going in to visit a big school to try and get the kids interested, always remembering that the Army Youth Team were not doing direct recruiting. Recruiting was a good job and an important job and I was pleased that I was doing it.

I was five years at CLRD and hardly anyone from the regiment, apart from Derek Hornblower, contacted me. Just before Christmas 1974, however, the RSM of the 4th Battalion, the territorial element of the Regiment, called me. They had their HQ in Davies Street, Mayfair. Now I knew the RSM; his name was John Wynne. He had passed through the depot when I was RSM there and he had been a CSM at that time. He said, 'Peter, sorry not to have been in touch with you sooner but as you will know I haven't been in situ very long. What are you doing?'

So I told him a bit about what I'd been doing since leaving Winchester.

Then he said, 'We're having a bit of a staff party here in Davies Street; why don't you come along to it? You're about the only Green Jacket in Central London. We should invite you. There are more than a few people here that you know so you can get up to date.'

Well, it sounded like a good idea to me and I went along. I had some good chats with a few of my old mates, and generally enjoyed myself. The commanding officer was Lieutenant Colonel John Holroyd and towards the end of the party he came to talk to me. He took me to one side.

'Ah,' he said, 'how long have you been doing this recruiting job?'

I told him that I'd been almost five years in Central London and that it suited me down to the ground, as it meant that I could stay in the army until I was fifty-five.

He asked me, 'Do you have to stay there? I'll tell you what has happened. The battalion has been given a new role; we are changing from home defence to BAOR [British Army Of Rhine] support reserve battalion. This means that our strength has been increased by an extra company and an additional officer called an admin officer is required, one which we have never had before. In fact I don't think anyone has heard of this role before. He'll be something between an adjutant and a quartermaster.'

'But you already have a quartermaster and an adjutant, Sir,' I replied.

'Yes,' he said, 'but this is something entirely different. It's a non-regular post but you're permanent staff. You are not a TA but neither are you a regular. You would be a Conrate officer and your engagement would be to the age of sixty.'

Well, this sounded very interesting. He continued, 'You get commissioned to the rank of captain straight away. Would you be interested?'

I thought, bloody hell, one of my fellow WO1s has been commissioned two years ago and is still a lieutenant, so I would be jumping over him. I said, 'Are you in a position to do this, Sir? I'm sorry, I'm not trying to belittle your authority or anything.'

He replied, 'Do I have the authority? I'm the bloody commanding officer; if I say you're coming, you're coming!'

I apologised, I had thought that it would have had to go higher up, but the CO clarified that he had been given the necessary authority. He explained that he had been told to find his own candidate and that is what he was doing. He added that he had the full backing of regimental headquarters for him to choose me. I told him that this was a bit of a shock, albeit a pleasant one, but I was more than interested. I also told him that being a QM had always been my ambition, but being knocked back in 1969, I thought I'd lost that chance.

He said, 'Go home and talk to Enid and in the meantime I'll find out all the details and get back to you.'

'This is not a wind up, is it, Colonel?' I said to him.

He replied, 'I don't do wind-ups. This is serious and you will fit in well here. I know you, and I know the other people here. So it's down to you.'

I got a message to go and see a retired officer in District HQ. He was an ex major whom I knew; he used to come into the sergeants' mess in CLRD some lunchtimes. He went through all the many things that I would have to do and the various responsibilities that I would have. To be honest it frightened me to death – when I saw how many jobs I was expected to do. I thought, God almighty, I'm taking a job that four or five people should be doing. Then he went through all the privileges that went with the role and all in all it looked like a good job. The CO of 4RGJ wanted me to start right away. It was early April 1975. I went to see the chief clerk of London District to arrange my transfer to 4RGJ and told him of my good fortune. He responded by saying, 'F***ing hell! Don't do it now; I've just applied for your Meritorious Service Medal for which you must have twenty-seven years regular service.'

'Bugger that, Bill, I'm going to be an officer,' I said.

He surprised me by saying, 'Yes, but you can have both. Ask your CO to delay your commissioning until the end of the month. You joined the army on 15 April 1948 and it's the 4th today so you will only have a couple of weeks to wait.'

So I contacted Lt. Col. Holroyd, who told me to go ahead and get my medal.

I was discharged from regular service on 27 April 1975 and commissioned as captain on 28 April 1975 – without a break in service.

CHAPTER 19

# A Commissioned Officer
# (1975–92)

O N 16 APRIL 1975 I qualified for the Meritorious Service Medal as authorised by the Records Office; to be published in the next routine orders. It would be presented in due course. And so I was commissioned into the 4th Battalion Royal Green Jackets as Captain Lawless 500047 in the position of Permanent Staff Admin Officer (PSAO) also referred to as Non Regular Permanent Staff (NRPS) in which I was to remain until I retired at sixty-two.

Once in role it really hit me as to how much work it entailed! My God it did. They hadn't had a PSAO before so the officers in Regimental HQ had had to undertake various admin jobs themselves. But with me there now things were different.

First of all they had a TA paymaster who was not a Regular officer so I had to take on all the Regulars' pay – leaving this officer as TA Paymaster of the battalion, but with me being the Imprest Holder. The Paymaster was Major Ian Hunter, who had been an officer in one of the Scottish Regiments and who had joined the TA after his Regular release. He was a lovely man, also a fellow Yorkshireman; we worked well together and became good friends.

Secondly, I became the PRI (President of the Regimental Institute) which meant looking after the welfare of the other rank soldiers: generally providing sporting equipment and suchlike, arranging for various grants to be made to certain requests for aid and maintaining all the accounts relating to welfare.

I also took over as treasurer of the officers' mess which also doubled as the Royal Green Jackets' London Club, although the Club was a separate entity. This was where the officers of the regiment, serving or retired, living or working in Central London could lunch and meet up. It didn't have any accommodation but could be booked for private parties, when available – military functions obviously had priority.

I was also responsible for the hiring and firing of all the civilian staff we had working in the battalion. This was quite a number, when you consider

125

that we didn't just have a battalion HQ in London. We also had companies in the Greater London area: Fulham, West Ham, Mile End and a company in the City. We also had companies in Oxford and Aylesbury with an offshoot in Bletchley. I started a system whereby the caretaker of each building became the barkeeper too. This gave them an additional bob or two and meant that I didn't have to employ anybody else.

On top of this I was also the married families' officer. This meant that I was responsible for ensuring that all the married regulars got an appropriate quarter. I also had to deal with any domestic situation that might arise. For example if Mrs Jones had just found out that her husband, Corporal Jones, had been sleeping around I would have to go and sort out the problem. I also became the Health and Safety Officer.

It began to occur to me that if there were any odd jobs that needed doing they would give them to me – 'give them to the new guy' seemed to be the idea. Well, I wasn't having this and it was brought to a head when the then training major wanted me to take over the responsibility of running the officers' mess. I had already taken over the officers' mess accounts and someone else had suggested that I might take on the MT (Motor Transport) officer role too. I'd had enough and would speak with the commanding officer. He had told me that if I ever wanted to speak to him I was just to knock on the door and walk in. However I decided to do this through official channels and arranged an interview through the adjutant.

And so I went to see the Colonel. I said, 'First of all, Colonel, I want to thank you for getting and giving me this job. I am delighted with it and it has given me the opportunity to stay in the army and particularly the regiment. When you arranged for me to go to see the major in District Headquarters I went through all the ins and outs of the job with him. He explained about the various responsibilities and tasks that would be within my scope, at the discretion of the commanding officer, and I was happy with that. But now I'm having jobs throw at me by every Tom, Dick, and Harry which are way outside my remit. I'm sure you will agree that I have enough to do, without being asked to take on jobs that should be done by other officers.'

He said, 'Peter [he called me by my Christian name now that I was an officer], I'm glad that we have got you here and already there are signs of where you have been and what you have been doing. Since you have been here, things are running more smoothly and I will make sure that you will only be asked to do what you are meant to do. But don't lose sight of the fact that I am the CO and I will decide who does what.'

I thanked him for listening to me, and added that I didn't mind helping out when necessary.

He replied, 'I know that. Keep up the good work.'

And that, as they say, was that. It took me about six months to settle down and get things sorted out as I wanted them. During this time I was ordered to attend at TAVR (Territorial and Volunteer Reserves) HQ in Duke of York Barracks on King's Road, Chelsea, to be presented by the Brigadier with my MSM; I was accompanied by my CO, John Holroyd.

I want to make quite clear that I did not carry out all these jobs personally as I had staff; clerical and practical. My clerical staff were civilians deployed from the civil service and consisted of two very good lady clerical officers, Miss Sandy Beesely and Mrs Beryl Lloyd. These two worked in my office dealing with typing, filing and general correspondence. Beryl used to also double with the battalion orderly room, Sandy was permanently with me. Sandy latterly also worked with financial matters, permanent staff pay and allowances. She was a godsend and remained loyal and enthusiastic during all my time. Other helpers came from the regular PSI sergeants, from signals, mortars and anti-tank. These PSIs all undertook different tasks under my supervision, such as visiting the other company locations and carrying out stock checks and reporting on accommodation stores. The mortar PSI was helpful with the PRI account and equipment. As manager of the London Club I had a mess sergeant and waiter, both regulars. Sergeant West was mess sergeant for about a ten-year spell. He was a bit stubborn at times but never let me down and always came up with the goods. Hence the Club had a great reputation within the regiment and elsewhere.

Perhaps the most helpful persons were the caretaker and his wife, Andrew and Marcelle Brogden. In addition to keeping the building safe and sound and well cleaned and maintained, they did other jobs such as managing the Riflemen's Bar, and assisting with all rank functions. They were a Godsend to me. Andrew was in the TA and over the years had gained promotion to CSM by the time I retired. Since then he has retired from the TA in the rank of Captain and we keep in touch on a regular basis.

When I was commissioned one of the terms of my contract was a non-entitlement to a married quarter, therefore we had to vacate our married quarter in Sweets Way. Enid and I decided to buy a property in the North London area. We spent about nine months in a flat in Quinta

127

Drive whilst we looked around. Finally we found a detached, two-bedroom bungalow in King Edward Road, New Barnet for £18,000. Enid and I were able to put down £5,000 as a deposit owing to the fact that, when I completed my twenty-seven years of Regular Service, I was awarded a full pension and a terminal (I hate that word) lump sum, tax free grant of £6,000. I had banked this and therefore was able to pay the deposit required and have sufficient funds to furnish the place. We took out a new type of mortgage – an endowment – which turned out to be a very good decision on our part. More on that later.

All the time we were in Sweets Way Enid had been working in the Royal Armoured Corps (RAC) Records Office which was also located in Whetstone. About the same time as I was coming to the end of my time in CLRD the RAC announced it was moving its Records Office to Chester and Enid was given the opportunity to relocate there with them. This happened before I was offered a commission so I still believed that I was going to have to leave the army when I reached fifty-five. It was a real quandary and we did seriously consider a move to Chester. As luck would have it, however, by the time the move actually took place I had been offered the PSAO job. In truth neither of us wanted to move away from Barnet where we had made so many wonderful friends so it was a relief not to have to do so. Enid soon found a job closer to home as a Clerical Officer with the Department of Social Services (DSS) who had an office in Barnet and after about three years, she was promoted to Executive Officer (EO) and posted to their Archway office. This was fine, for by now Ian, our elder son, had moved out to live with some mates in town. Later he started courting Linda and they got married in 1979.

Graham our other son was now firmly settled in Queen Elizabeth (QE) Boys School, approaching sixteen and thinking about leaving and getting a job. In any case he was old enough to look after himself at home after school until either Enid or I came home. Incidentally, Graham, was now being called by another Christian name by his schoolmates, just as Ian had in earlier years; it was 'Harvey'. This had come about because his school had done a take-off of the film of the same name which included an invisible rabbit called Harvey. Harvey, aka Graham, was the rabbit and his school mates insisted that he be called 'Harvey' ever after because when anything wanted doing he became invisible!

Graham broke his leg whilst playing football and was off school for a time and Enid's mother came to stay with us. One day she was in with Graham when one of his mates from school knocked at the door and Gladys opened it – Enid and I were at work. The young fellow asked how Harvey was whereupon Gladys told the lad that he had got the wrong house – she didn't know about Graham's nickname – and the boy didn't know Graham by any other name than Harvey. The confusion was eventually cleared up by Graham himself; he had been listening to the conversation and was laughing his side sore.

In 1980 Graham married Tina, just one year after his elder brother's marriage. Graham had left school at sixteen and a half and got a job in the West End at a milliner's owned by an ex Green Jackets officer called Max Glazier. Max was a frequent visitor to the London Club and in discussion with him one lunchtime I happened to mention about Graham wanting a job. He asked me how old he was and I said, 'Sixteen.' He said, 'Send him to see me,' which I duly did. Graham went by himself, refusing to have me go with him. He got the job and from there moved from hats to clothing by joining J. Dege & Son in Saville Row, from where he has prospered, and now is near to having his own business.

Meanwhile Ian had progressed from being a tea taster to become a sugar importer for Tate & Lyle, for Tate & Lyle had bought out Ridgeway's. Later acting on an advertisement Ian applied for an assistant manager's job with the Gateway Building Society; he got the job and was eventually installed in their City Branch. So he'd given up tea and sugar for finance. During this time he was making friends with various cricketing people as he was a cricketer himself and played for Southgate Compton, a North London team. He undertook to organise certain functions for professional cricketers that were having their benefit year, particularly those from the northern counties. This voluntary role meant arranging dinners down in the south – acting as their agent, as it were. One of the people who he did this for was Martin Moxon, a Yorkshire cricketer. Martin was selected to go on the England tour of India and he asked Ian if he would like to go with him. Ian said he would love to and managed to get time off from work on the understanding that he wrote a few words about the tour to be published in the Gateway magazine. Ian did this and a jolly good job he made of it too. This was the start of a number of dinners that Ian organised, all of which I was invited to and most of which I attended. He did one for Geoffrey Boycott (another Yorkshire player), another for Arnold Sidebottom (whose son is now playing for England) and one or two others including David Gower – all first class cricketers.

Remember I mentioned in an earlier chapter how delighted Enid's father Bill was when Ian was born. This was because the little chap would qualify to play cricket for Yorkshire – having been born in Yorkshire. Well, indeed this did happen because Martin Moxon and Geoffrey Boycott and a couple of other players asked Ian if he would like to play in a friendly game against Tring in Berkshire. This was always played after the last country game of the season – which was nearly always against Essex. Well, Ian was delighted and did play in this game. I can still hear the announcement over the loudspeaker saying, 'Coming in number six is Ian Lawless of Yorkshire.' So Ian did get to play for Yorkshire and I was very proud of this, as I know his grandfather would have been too.

In 1975 coinciding with my commission to captain, I was appointed as a Director of the North Middlesex Golf Club and as such became a member of the Entertainments Committee, now known as the Social Committee. We had a number of members who when pushed were good entertainers. Perhaps the most professional of these 'entertainers' was Tim Voss, a past Captain, whose musical knowledge was outstanding. He also played the trumpet, was brilliant on the piano and could read and write music to a very high standard: a most useful chap to have when you are organising club shows – of which we produced plenty. These included a World War One musical, *The End of the Pier Show*, and *North Mid Muppet Show*, all of which were presented and performed by club members. Other social events included candlelit suppers on the last Friday in each month. These were limited to forty people, so you can imagine the competition for a place. We had novelty dance evenings and fancy dress parties with the odd Tramps Ball thrown in. I must say that with our experience of such events through the officers' mess functions, Enid and I were leading lights in all the do's and we loved every moment. We had a good Social Committee Chairman in Henry Mcfayden, 'Mac' to his friends. He had a great organising brain but couldn't act for toffee. A good chap!

I will mention just one show – it was an old time music hall show. Lots of the acts were performed like the old originals, doing the things that they did. Some very good impressions were performed. Enid and I decided to do the song by Joyce Grenfell, 'Stately as a Galleon', but we also decided that we would incorporate a dance act to this, despite the fact that Enid had been having problems with her left knee for some time. I was going to be Mrs Tiverton to Enid's Mrs Fanshaw for which I had to dress as a woman and in a balldress too. Enid, of course, provided the clothing but

*34. Stately as a Galleon – Enid and Peter (on the right)*

unfortunately her shoes didn't fit me, so we had to go out and buy some. As we walked down the High Street in Barnet we went into the Help the Aged shop. There were no other customers in there and after looking round the various shelves Enid spotted a pair of gold dance shoes. She said, 'Try these on; they look about your size.'

So I took off my shoes and tried them on. They were very tight and I said so.

Enid replied, 'They will be OK when you have your tights on.'

I could see the shop assistant watching us so I said to her, 'They are for a fancy dress party,' and she replied, 'They all say that.' We got the shoes and quickly left. How embarrassing!

Another embarrassing moment was at the golf club on the night of the show. I was in the men's dressing room changing for our act – the dressing rooms are on the first floor – when Enid shouted up in a loud voice, 'Peter, don't forget to go to the toilet before you put your tights on.' All the golf club heard her and the laugher didn't stop for a good five minutes.

These were just a few of the many memories I have of the social occasions that we enjoyed so much at North Mid.

*35. North Middlesex Club Captain 1984*

Life was pretty good. I was playing lots of golf and improving my handicap; the lowest I got down to was 7 but found this difficult to play to. The longest time I spent on any one handicap was 9. When I went up to 10 I became eligible to play for the Foxes – those with a handicap between 10 and 19. I became Foxes' Captain in 1983 and a few years later I was made Foxes' League President, a post I held for three years.

I was asked to be vice Captain of North Middlesex Golf Club in 1983 and became Club Captain in 1984. I was very honoured to be asked.

I was still serving all this time and a couple of years before I became Club Captain I was promoted to major. This came about because much of my work involved liaison with HQ London District, particularly to do with pay and accounts, dealing mainly with majors and above. Being a captain I was not always listened to, and was being put to one side, so I spoke to my commanding officer, Lt. Col. Nigel Mogg (he later became a brigadier) and suggested that if he could make me a local major this would give me a bit more clout with the District HQ. He agreed and it worked out quite nicely. I received no extra pay but I did keep my rank until the end of my service.

When I had my Club Captain's annual dinner at the golf club I invited my then commanding officer, Lt. Col. Peter Lyddon[4] to be my principal guest. When he rose to speak at the end of dinner, the first thing he said was, 'I think that this is a unique occasion, for, as far as I know this is the first time that a major has been promoted to captain. It's usually the other way around!'

Meanwhile, in 1983 Linda gave birth to our first grandchild, Sarah. This event caused the new great-grandmother Gladys once more to descend upon us. She went to stay with Ian and Linda and was of tremendous help. Three years later their second daughter Emma, was born in September. In April of that year, Tina had Kelly. Now both our sons had children, three lovely granddaughters for Enid to dote on, as she certainly did.

In 1993, Enid and I bought a timeshare apartment in Portugal. It was in the Alto Golf and Country Club near Alvor which is located between Portimo and Lagos. We initially bought one week, with a view to me taking my mates golfing every year, as the price included country membership of the club's golf course. On the first visit, however, Enid decided to come along too. We both enjoyed it so much that when we discovered that the week preceding the one I had already purchased was still free, we bought that too, so we had the seventh and eighth weeks of each succeeding year. When we couldn't go at that particular time, which wasn't often, we would exchange those two weeks and go somewhere else – this wasn't necessarily in Portugal but almost anywhere in the world. We invariably took family and friends with us to the Alto Club, and generally made very good use of this facility.

I have so many good memories of Portugal that I cannot recount them all here but one that sticks with me is parring the 16th on the Alto course the first time I played it. Although this hole is now billed as the longest par 5 in Europe it used to be a par 6. There was a shield in the club house for recording any birdies on the hole. It was empty when I parred it and, years later when we eventually gave it up, it was still empty – it was a formidable hole.

Initially I played every day when in Portugal but as time went on I divided my time more equally between my golf and other social activities. Although Enid didn't play golf I did manage to coax her into driving the

---

[4]Peter Lyddon later became a Brigadier and on his retirement from the army he became a Chapter Clerk and then Chapter Steward in York Minster.

golf buggy on the odd occasion. I always say this was so she could join me for a meal afterward and had nothing to do with the convenience of having a driver for the round!

Perhaps you are wondering at this point why Enid didn't play golf. After all she had been very sporty in her youth and a very skilful korfball player as I've previously mentioned. Well, in truth I think Enid was rather a fool to herself in many ways. She had this adamant attitude towards things – nobody was going to tell her what to do. Not long after I had joined North Mid, Enid and I were at a social function sitting with a couple of long standing members called Jean and Harold Cramb. Now whilst I could get on with anyone Enid liked to reserve judgement until she got to know them a little better. As any non-playing spouse of a golfer knows, one of the first questions you get asked is, 'Do you play golf?' So I was not surprised to hear Jean ask that very question of Enid.

She answered, 'Oh no. My husband plays but I don't,' and Jean, bless her, replied with, 'Oh well, you will.'

To which Enid emphatically responded with 'Oh no I bloody well won't.' And she stuck to that. She did however enjoy putting when we were in Portugal and got very excited when she got a 'hole in one'.

Back in London my job with the 4th Battalion was made considerably easier by the introduction of admin. officers to each company. I, being the senior officer, now had my own little 'admin. officer army'. Needless to say this took a load of work away from me. The responsibility was still there but the workload decreased.

This situation now allowed me to pay more attention to social matters; which came within the remit of my job. I decided to instigate an annual Permanent Staff day out at the Derby. This started with a champagne breakfast at our Fulham Drill Hall, then on by coach to Epsom. The coach had a bar on board and lots of food packed away ready for consumption, both before and after the racing. At Christmas I also organised the Permanent Staff party just before we broke up for the holiday.

Other events that took place during my service there were when the 4th Battalion was presented with the Freedom of the City of Westminster; what jollifications we had then. The Officers' Ball lasted throughout the night with a kedgeree breakfast at 5 a.m.

On a personal note, Enid and I received an invitation to a Royal Palace Garden Party. I borrowed a top hat and morning suit and the commanding officer lent us his staff car and driver. What a lovely day and a great honour.

36. My own little 'admin. officer army'

37. Waiting for the staff car to take us to the Palace

135

In the Palace gardens I was approached by none other than lieutenant-commander Tim Laurence whom I had met when he was serving on HMS *Alacrity* and I was a guest at the ship's officer's party and chatted to him as he was also a keen golfer. Later at a reciprocal party at our mess in Davies Street we again exchanged golfing stories and it ended with Tim inviting me to play in a tournament at Tidworth Golf Club which unfortunately I was not able to attend. Now Tim was equerry to Her Majesty and he took us under his wing and steered us towards Prince Michael of Kent where I was able to remind him that we had met when he was an officer cadet at Sandhurst.

The main pleasure I got from the job was attending annual camp. This is the time that the whole battalion get together in one central place and practise their warlike skills – indeed the only time the CO can actually command his battalion in the field. The locations of the annual camp were diverse; Otterburn in Northumberland was my first camp. At camp, because of my position in the battalion, I had no war role but in my job as PRI I organised a soldiers' canteen with a bar. This was not time consuming because once I had set it up it virtually ran itself, so I was able to take advantage of this and explore the surrounding area – it was like being on holiday. We held our annual camp at Otterburn three times during my time and I often played golf at Bellingham (9-holes) and at Hexham whilst the battalion was there.

Other places the battalion held annual camp, during my time, were Brecon in Wales, twice on the Isle of Man and three times to Vogelsang in Germany – where I had chopped wood in 1948 during Operation Woodpecker – also in Oakhampton, Devon, the Isle of Mull in Scotland and twice more in Germany for full deployment in a major exercise as they would be in a war situation. On these two occasions there was no permanent place to stay and no job for me, except I went to stay with a regular unit and acted like a NAAFI wagon with fags, soft drinks and cake and biscuits. The point I'm trying to make is that annual camp to me was like a perk, holidaying in these different places where I might never had normally visit.

I spent in all seventeen years in Davies Street and I like to think that I was of some assistance to the seven different commanding officers and numerous quartermasters, adjutants, training majors and loads of regular other ranks doing a tour of duty in the TA. Being established in such a position for such a long time meant that I knew the who, when and where of things. I knew how to get things done and could help those new to their jobs to get settled in.

Shortly before we retired, Enid was diagnosed with diabetes. This initially wasn't a problem but in later years it did interfere with her general health. Little known to me then, I was going to have my fair share of health issues too. Already I had had to have a knee replacement and was diagnosed with arthritis which was affecting my perambulatory joints.

I eventually retired in 1992 at the age of sixty-two. Enid, who had been in the Civil Service for twenty years, retired six months later.

Unbeknown to me, the commanding officer, Lt. Col. Jamie Daniels, had organised a collection for me and had circulated it to all the other officers in the regiment, asking for a donation. He had collected sufficient not only to buy me a full set of Hogan Edge golf clubs of the very highest quality, but also to enough to present Enid with a limited edition porcelain figurine of a 43rd officer, circa 1812 – which still holds pride of place on our mantelpiece. We were flabbergasted and touched by everyone's generosity.

I am still using those clubs today.

Finally Enid and I were dined out by the officers' mess – a tearful occasion, for both of us.

**Major Peter Lawless**

Peter finally retired on 16th January 1992 after 43 years service having first enlisted in the 43rd and 52nd on 15th April 1948. All those members of the regiment who served with him or knew him will not be surprised to know that he intends to keep himself fully occupied, even if it's only with a brand new set of golf clubs presented to him by the 4th Battalion which he served as loyally for almost 17 years.

Here is his letter of appreciation:

66 King Edward Road
New Barnet
Herts
EN5 5AU
Tel : 081-449-1819

Please accept my apologies for this collective acknowledgement. At my farewell dinner I was presented with a magnificent set of Hogan Edge golf clubs together with other gifts, in particular, a superb china figurine presented to Enid. After the initial shock and embarrassment at the magnitude of the presents, it eventually struck home how tremendous the response must have been to Jamie Daniell's "begging letter". I wish to thank everyone who contributed and I am deeply grateful to you all for your generous donations. The golf clubs are superb and my handicap will, no doubt, soon start plummeting.

I value greatly all the very many friends and acquaintances I have made over the years and earnestly hope that I can continue to support the Regiment and its activities.

With sincere humility
Peter Lawless

PART 3

Civvi Street

CHAPTER 20

# What now?

IN THE YEARS AFTER RETIREMENT nothing of any great significance took place. At first I couldn't understand the civvie way of life, and it took me a long time to settle down. With no military commitments I was now free to attend more golf meetings than heretofore. I had joined the Truants Golf Society in 1986 but had found it very difficult to attend the mandatory four meetings each year. Now I was no longer working I could attend all the Truants' meetings and, these together with the four annual London Golf Captain's meetings, gave me plenty of golf. It didn't stop there; for as well as the club competitions at weekends I became a member of the 'dirty dozen', twelve club members who had a week's golfing each year at various places throughout the UK and indeed Ireland and France. We played mainly on championship courses some of which I had had to miss due to my military commitments but I was now free to go on all of them.

Now I can see that this might appear to you that I was being a bit callous and uncaring about Enid's health situation but not so. Over this time Enid was fully supportive of my golf activities; indeed when I suggested that I should stay with her, she insisted that I go and not hang around getting under her feet acting like an 'old mother hen' as she put it. She didn't just end up having a replacement knee; she also had lots of trouble with her legs and feet, particularly with her toes. This came to a head when the diabetic chiropodist that Enid was seeing on a regular basis pricked a blister she had on one toe and the damn thing became septic and then gangrenous and had to be amputated. Almost a month after this she had to have two more toes removed from the same foot. This meant being admitted as an inpatient and this was the start of a number of hospital stays. Nevertheless she never let this get her down and she was the first to decide where we should go when I suggested a holiday.

Even with our respective health issues Enid and I did manage to fit in at least one holiday per year but in February 1996 our twenty year mortgage came to an end and changed our horizons. You may remember that we bought our bungalow in King Edward Road in 1976. We took out an endowment mortgage, all the rage back then but not very popular nowadays. However for Enid and me it was a good investment; after only having to pay off the interest on a monthly basis we received a cheque for £37,000 when it matured. So there we were with the sum of £24,000 after paying off the original mortgage amount of £13,000. Quite a windfall, as we'd both forgotten all about this.

We decided to have one final fling and enjoy ourselves whilst we still could. Being realistic we knew, with our various health problems, that long trips away from home were likely to become more difficult as time went by. We went to our timeshare operator RCI and asked if we could 'bank' two year's worth of our timeshare allotment: four weeks in total. We then asked them if they could help us plan a trip that would enable us to visit all the places in the world that we hadn't visited whilst I was in the army; which wasn't many as you will have gathered from previous chapters.

Enid and I went up to RCI's headquarters in Kettering and met with a very helpful young lady who worked with us to put together an itinerary. She asked us how long we wanted to be away and we told her that we weren't quite sure. Enid and I were still outpatients at the hospital and we both needed to get our all-clears before we could embark on our trip.

So we decided to go for it – a world tour – yes, why not. Bugger it! It didn't matter what happened back home and if we got ill we would just have to get treatment abroad.

It started with Australia, somewhere we had never been. When I was serving in Singapore I had planned to take local leave and visit Australia instead of coming home to the UK. It was a popular destination for many servicemen and their families and they would take two weeks' leave to visit and that's what we had planned to do. But we delayed our decision and by the time we had got around to thinking about it seriously, the regiment were posted back to Berlin and the opportunity was lost. Now we had another chance.

We also had a good friend in Perth, Margaret Todd, and we planned to drop in and surprise her. If we were going to Australia then it made sense to visit New Zealand too. I happened to mention this to Dr Diane Smith, the lady who I had won North Mid's Arthur Lord Mixed Competition[5] with in 1977. Diane was from New Zealand and when I mentioned we were going to spend a week there, she was horrified. 'A week,' she said,

---

[5]Arthur Lord was a founder member of North Middlesex Golf Club. When he had to resign from his Presidency in 1936 owing to ill health the President's Mixed Foursomes was renamed the Arthur Lord Mixed Foursomes as a tribute to his contribution to the club.

'you want a year to do it justice; it's lovely.' I compounded the problem by admitting that we had planned to spend four weeks in Australia. 'You don't need four weeks in Australia,' she retorted, 'it's all the same thing!' It was very useful however to have Diane recommend some 'must see' places that we should plan into our itinerary whilst in New Zealand.

One thing led to another. We had heard about this train journey in Canada and in planning to do this it seemed sensible to have a stop-over from New Zealand in Hawaii. So this is how our world trip started to take shape. We would fly east and circumnavigate the globe, returning from the west. We spent over a year planning the trip with the help of RCI, who I have to say were wonderful. We had such fun looking through the brochures they sent us and mulling over their suggested itineraries. In the end it worked out that we would be away for nine weeks.

We paid for everything up front and the whole trip cost around £12,000 excluding spending money. It was the largest amount of money I had ever handed over in one lump and I would be lying if I said I wasn't a little nervous as I did so. And as the departure date approached both Enid and I were worried that the trip would not live up to our expectations. A worry, as it turned out, that was completely unfounded.

It was in 1996 that Enid got the all clear from her consultant, Dr Alex Loh. I having had a knee replacement was now having the trouble with my hips, as I mentioned earlier, but decided that I could put up with a little discomfort for the duration of the trip and deal with any fall-out when we got back.

And so on Tuesday 22 October 1996 we left for Heathrow airport and our long anticipated world tour began.

CHAPTER 21

# Our world tour

I T WAS EXCITING STUFF.

We were taken to Heathrow Airport by Ron Mullings; Ron and his wife Nora were good friends of ours who had been to Ireland with us on a number of occasions which I will mention later. Ron had just retired from his job as a chauffeur so it seemed only right and proper that he drive Enid and me to the airport!

We set off on our adventure from Heathrow terminal 3 at about midday on Tuesday 22 October 1996. We were on our way to Australia but had a one night stop-over in Singapore. It was a long flight and we were glad to be met by a car at the airport and taken to our hotel. When planning our trip RCI had struggled to find a car to pick us up but had finally succeeded and both Enid and I were so pleased that we had insisted on this. We stayed at the Riverview Hotel on the banks of the Singapore River close to Clarke Quay but we didn't have much time to look around as we had to check in for our flight to Perth early the next morning. That didn't matter as both Enid and I had been to Singapore before.

Our flight from Singapore to Australia got us into Perth mid afternoon the next day, Thursday 24 October. Although the flight wasn't all that long we had decided to stay one night at Sullivans Hotel in Perth before travelling on to the timeshare complex we were to stay at for six nights. It was called the Silver Sands Resort, one hour's drive south of Perth on the coast at a place called Mandurah.

Although we'd spent a long time deciding where we would stop on our grand tour we chose not to have a detailed schedule to follow. We both felt that waiting until we arrived was a far more sensible approach. In the end we did fall into a sort of routine; having settled in to the resort and found our way around its facilities we paid a visit to the information desk and asked the locals to make recommendations for us to choose from. This worked perfectly. In Perth we ended up doing a number of excursions which all ended up being to places that ended with an 'up' – like 'Yonderup' or 'Dwellingup'.

I mentioned previously that we had a friend who lived in Perth:

Margaret Todd. Margaret and her husband had emigrated six years earlier to be with their daughter who had married an Australian. Sadly, Philip, her husband, had died in the meantime but we did get to meet up and indeed catch up with Margaret. What we did was arrange to take Margaret out for a meal the night before we departed for Melbourne, the next stop on our itinerary. We had arranged to come back to the city centre and stay overnight in the same hotel as before so that we could do this. We did! Then we left the next day and flew to Melbourne on the south-east coast of Australia.

As we flew to Melbourne we travelled through four time zones. Time passes fast enough on its own without it being further speeded up by these invisible boundaries! We arrived none the worse for our ordeal and were met by a car which took us to the Nepean Country Club Resort where we spent the next six nights. The Nepean is situated in the heart of Mornington Peninsula at a place called Rosebud.

Again we asked the reception what sort of things we should see whilst we were there.

The staff really knew how to make their guests feel special. They were able to give us loads of suggestions as to what we should visit and also put on social events so that everyone on the complex could get to know each other: singing and dancing and suchlike. Enid and I really enjoyed ourselves.

Lo and behold and quite by accident we discovered that the Melbourne Cup was on during our stay. Now I suppose the Melbourne Cup is the Australian equivalent of Ascot or Derby Day in the UK. What a wonderful coincidence and although we had been quite oblivious of this fact when booking our stay in Melbourne we were lucky enough to get tickets. A coach took us to and from the event and we had a marvellous time. Enid and I had been to the Derby many times in England but we'd seen nothing like this; it was splendid and one of the highlights of our tour.

Another trip the resort suggested was to visit the little penguins on Phillip Island. We took an organised tour to see them all waddle ashore – it was a fantastic sight. They came ashore in groups of fifty or sixty strong and then milled around on the beach, as if they were behind the starting tape at the Grand National. And then suddenly as if the starter had fired his pistol they all started moving inland to their nesting sites – truly amazing.

We met an American couple whilst we were there who were also keen golfers and so it was only natural that I play a round with them at the local

*38. View over Melbourne Cup Racecourse*

*39. Fairy penguins coming ashore on Phillip Island*

course. I would have liked to have played at the Royal Melbourne Golf Club but you needed a member's introduction for that, so I had to be content with just a drive by.

After making another trip to visit to 'Arthur's Seat', a chairlift journey to a lovely place, all too soon our stay in Melbourne came to an end and we flew to Sydney. When we arrived we made our own way to another Sullivans Hotel (now the Arts Hotel) on Oxford Street, Paddington, south of the city; so we felt right at home! Sydney was more recognisable as a city, with tall buildings like Centrepoint which is Sydney's tallest free standing structure. We did visit this, twice. We'd found out that the tower had a revolving restaurant, said to have spectacular views, so we decided to have lunch there one day. We got talking to a local man who told us that the best views were to be had at dusk when you could watch Sydney 'light up', so we just had to go back for dinner too, so that we could see this and it was well worth it. From our vantage point we spotted a place called Grace Brothers and some wag had written next to the sign, 'Are you being served?'

We found out that, with respect to sightseeing, everything seemed to happen at a place called Circular Quay; coach and boat trips started and ended there, as did most public transport. As it happened this wasn't very far from our hotel and so we didn't need a car to get around. The famous Opera House and the fantastic Sydney Harbour Bridge could be viewed in all their splendour from this point too. We did a lot of trips both by coach and by boat; many recommended, again, by the very helpful hotel staff.

Enid and I were not able to get out into the real 'bush' but that didn't matter because we got to see a lot of the local wildlife by visiting the many parks around Sydney. I have a number of photos with Enid cuddling a koala and equally as many with her turning her head away from a snake; she couldn't stand snakes.

We did a great trip up into the Blue Mountain, to Katoomba. We saw the magnificent Three Sisters rock formation and took the Skyway across Jamison Valley with its impressive views. This trip was on 11 November and on the way at exactly 11 o'clock the coach driver pulled into the roadside, handed out poppies to everyone and we had a two minutes silence. I was impressed as to how seriously the Australian's took Armistice Day.

We also took a guided coach tour to the capital of Australia, Canberra, specially built for the purpose of governing. Our guide was excellent – very knowledgeable. Everything is built on a huge scale – the government buildings had two enormous fountains outside. There was an excellent war museum there, covering their military history right up to modern day which I particularly enjoyed.

We couldn't leave Sydney without visiting the famous Bondi beach although neither of us did any surfing! What a wonderful stretch of sand. It's so massive it never gets full. The coaches went right down to the sand so Enid and I were able to dip our toes into the Tasman Sea. And of course it was November but rather odd to see advertisements for Christmas, with false ice and snow; it was hot and sunny – not at all Christmassy.

After seven fabulous nights in Sydney we had to drag ourselves away to continue our holiday and we flew north to Cairns where we stayed at the Paradise Village Resort. All our plans were going like clockwork. The resort was at Buchan Point just north of Cairns itself, right on the shore of the Coral Sea. It was magical. We had paid a great deal of money for this holiday and, as I mentioned before, were a little worried that things wouldn't live up to our expectations. However all our anxieties were swept away and even Enid, bless her, enjoyed bathing and sunning herself on these magnificent shores.

Going on trips all the time is quite tiring and we had decided to take it easy and relax and sun ourselves in this tropical paradise. We did get lured into doing a couple of trips that were recommended as 'must dos' whilst we were there. One was to the Kuranda Rainforest by skyrail cableway and train – again spectacular views – where a little town had been built which certainly gave us some respite from the heat. The town appeared to be in the middle of nowhere but we did pass a number of stations on the way up. It intrigued me, where the people on the platforms had come from. The other trip was to the Great Barrier Reef. We took a ferry out to a place called Dunk Island where we picked up our tour boat. It was like an ordinary sailing ship but with glass sides so we could see more. When we started out there was nothing to see but all of a sudden you could see a submerged green forested land and we were asked to look out for various fish and to encourage them to swim around the boat the captain threw shrimp and things into the water. Immediately there was a frenzy of fish of ever increasing sizes as the larger ones chased the smaller ones away. There was a line of rocks going all round the coast four to six miles out from the mainland. The sea was so clear we had great views down onto the coral reef.

My main memory of Australia was the clear blue skies, lack of pollution

*40. Up via Skyrail cablecar*

*41. Enid and me in Kuranda market*

*42. Down by train*

and fantastic views: not the hustle and bustle of the UK. It was certainly turning into the holiday of a lifetime.

Eventually our time in 'paradise' came to an end and we flew to Brisbane to catch a connecting flight to Auckland in New Zealand. We passed through another three time zones and so arrived late at night. We stayed at a travel lodge by the airport and picked up a hire car the next morning. Enid and I then made our own way to Club Paihia in the Bay of Islands on the east coast of New Zealand's North Island.

We moved into our timeshare and again the staff at the resort gave us advice as to what we should see. We already had a great view from our villa as it was located on top of a hill. Although we had a car we did book a couple of coach trips. We did one trip that was focused on New Zealand's heritage and the relationship with the indigenous Maori people. We visited a museum where there was an impressive 35-yard long war canoe that held eighty warriors.

We went out on a trip around the bay itself which included passage through the iconic 'Hole in the Rock'. The peninsula where this 'hole' was was covered in millions of birds but Enid and I were more concerned with

*43. London only 10,498 nautical miles*

how the captain was going to negotiate our boat through the said 'hole'. We survived as have many others before and after us so I guess it wasn't as perilous as it looked! Dolphins accompanied us most of the way.

We did another coach trip to Cape Regina and its famous lighthouse: the most northerly point of the North Island and a sacred place for the Maori people. Here there is a signpost, like you would see in the British countryside, with distances to the major cities in the world, London being 10,498 nautical miles – a long way from home. We travelled back along the 90 Mile Beach – an amazingly long stretch of beach which isn't actually 90 miles long but no matter. We passed some tall sand dunes where we saw people tobogganing down them – it looked exhilarating but a hard slog back up to the top for another go. If it wasn't for that I would have had a go myself!

Kiwis of course are nocturnal animals and on the endangered species list. You would be very lucky to see one in the wild these days although environmentalists are working hard to reintroduce them and I wish them every success. Their plight is due to the possum, introduced from Australia at the turn of the twentieth century. Ironically whilst the possum was a pest in Australia, their culling has been so successful that they are now on the

*44. Sunrise over Haleakala volcano*

endangered list there themselves. No such luck in New Zealand however. Enid and I got to see these odd creatures in a nature reserve where their day is reversed by artificial lighting so that visitors can see them moving around. This is why you are asked not to take flash photos. However I have to own up to taking one flash photo myself – I expect the kiwi I captured on film thought it was lightning!

Although we had a fabulous time in the Bay of Islands we decided to cut short our stay there so that we could go and visit Rotorua. Rotorua is an active volcanic area where hot mud bubbles in pools and geezers spurt out huge plumes of hot water and steam. One we saw was called Prince of Wales' Feathers. In fact we heard that the locals use washing powder to encourage one particularly large geezer to erupt at prearranged times so no tourist is disappointed!

New Zealand was spellbinding; we had a wonderful time and would not had missed it for all the world and wished we could have stayed longer (as my Arthur Lord partner, Dr Diane Smith had suggested back at North Mid during our planning stage) and seen some of the South Island. However, it was time to move on.

The night before we left we invited two old friends, Fay and John Cocker, to dinner at our hotel. They now lived south of Auckland. I had met John when he was a WO1 at the New Zealand Embassy when I was a recruiter in London District and had been in correspondence with him and his wife ever since they left England. He was one of the three other people I took down to Winchester to see a passing out parade. We had a lovely evening catching up.

The next afternoon we drove to Auckland Airport and flew to Maui, Hawaii via Honolulu. On this flight we crossed the International Date Line so we left Auckland on 17:15 on Thursday 28 November and arrived in Honolulu at 4:45 in the morning of the same day! So we made up some of that time I had complained about losing earlier from our holiday and gained almost a whole additional day.

We stayed for one night at a hotel near the airport in Maui. That turned out to be very fortuitous as there was a bit of a do laid on that evening by the hotel. It was a kind of BBQ but with entertainment which was very nice indeed: Hawaiian dancing girls. I didn't need much encouragement to get up and dance with one of the girls which I greatly enjoyed. We really had a good time with lots of fun and laughter.

The next morning we collected our car and drove to the Kuleana Club timeshare. Our apartment wasn't ready because we were a little early but that didn't matter because we were able to sit by the beach and enjoy the view. We had been so lucky with our timeshares. Our timeshare in Portugal was a two-bedded en-suite affair so that meant everywhere we went on this holiday we got the equivalent, which was great – we could really spread out. There was a wonderful pool at the Club too. Of course Hawaii is part of the United States which we had to keep reminding ourselves about.

Maui has the largest volcano on the Hawaiian Islands, Haleakala. At 3a.m. we took a coach trip to the top of this volcano – now extinct – to see the sun rise. We took blankets because at 10,000 ft, as you can imagine, before sunrise it was pretty chilly. It was superb, cold but magical! Before the sun actually rose the horizon was lit up with all different colours; purples, red and oranges and even greens; it was absolutely fantastic. I had my camera on continuous shutter so that I could capture this amazing sequence of events. Eventually the sun lit up the crater itself and that was amazing too – what a view from the top.

It is hard to believe that later that same day we were some 100 ft below sea level watching the Hawaiian sea life from a submarine called *Atlantis*.

*45.  10,000 ft and 37°F*

*46.  to  − 100 ft and 85°F!*

From almost freezing to death whist waiting for sunrise we had returned to a much more pleasant 85 degrees Fahrenheit. I don't know whether it was because we were under the water rather than on it but this trip proved to be far more successful than the one we took to the Great Barrier Reef in Australia. We saw a far greater variety of marine life, including a manta ray, at much closer quarters and we also got to see much more of the coral reef. Hawaii did seem like a real paradise: fantastic beaches, wonderful hospitality and a perfect climate. All too soon it was time to leave.

We flew to Vancouver in Canada from Honolulu. This is where the warm clothing we had packed and lugged around with us all this time was going to come in useful. The temperature in the Hawaiian Islands averages around 80 degrees Fahrenheit but the temperature in Vancouver at 7:30 in the morning was a bracing 37 degrees.

Having had a good five hours sleep on the plane we weren't the slightest bit tired when we arrived so once we had checked into our hotel we took a coach tour around the city. Of course a tour like this can only give you highlights of what the city has to offer. Enid and I were sure that there was a great deal more to see both from a cultural and a historical perspective and we kind of half promised each other that we would have to come back another time to do it justice but we never did.

That evening we had a super meal in the hotel where Enid and I had our first (and last!) taste of sushi – as we discovered it was all raw fish we weren't bothered too much with that! On returning to our room we had one final treat in store: a fantastic view of Vancouver City by night.

I think the main highlight of our whole trip was our journey from Vancouver to Toronto on the Via Rail Train. Although we had booked first class tickets we were slightly disappointed with our cabin; it was rather small. However, when I discovered that there were only eleven passengers in first class I asked whether we could have two adjoining compartments, one for living and one for sleeping. The answer was yes of course you can but you'll have to pay more money. Off I went to the ticket office to sort this out and we ended up with a wonderful living space with our own steward who looked after us as if we were royalty; it was an absolutely luxurious trip. Almost as soon as we left Vancouver the train started to climb and the mountains came into view. Even though it was 10 o'clock at night there was still quite a bit of light and we were treated to some magnificent views right from the start and being the middle of winter there was snow everywhere.

*47. Via Rail Train – first view of the Rockies*

Enid and I were a little worried that we wouldn't be able to sleep on the train because of the movement and noise but in fact it had the opposite effect; the train literally rocked us to sleep and we both had a great night. The one slight downside to the trip was that Enid's leg started to play up. I guess we had been on our feet a lot during our travels and it was lucky that whilst on the train the only walking we had to do was to walk from our compartment to the first class dining car – and we were able to manage that!

As I said there were only eleven of us in first class and with our own bar we were able to get to know them all quite well over the three-day journey. One couple were South Africans, another pair came from America and the others were Canadian. One Canadian chap we met ran an electrical firm in Toronto but was also buying into a business in Bletchley, Buckinghamshire – it's a small world. He had his secretary with him, or that was how the young lady was introduced to us. They were sharing a cabin so I don't think I need say more about that! Anyway as we were talking over an after dinner drink this guy – I think his name was John Black – happened to mention a monologue he had seen on the TV. He couldn't quite remember what it was called but it was something with a 'lion' in it. Immediately Enid said, 'Oh you mean "Albert and the Lion" by Stanley Holloway.'

'Oh is that what it it's called?' he said, 'well, I thought it was very funny.'

Enid said, 'Would you like to hear it then?' You see she knew it off by heart because it was one of the monologues that she had recited at the golf club. So Enid performed it there and then. Of course the rest of the carriage couldn't help but hear it too and after she had finished she got a round of applause and much praise. We all got on so well that I decide to buy everyone port that evening. The next night when we came in for dinner there was wine on the table. Our Canadian friend John had bought it. I mentioned something about buying more port after dinner only to be informed that another couple had decided it would be brandy this evening and they were buying that. And this is how things went on for the whole trip; it was really great.

The journey wasn't a continuous one; we stopped twice: once at Jasper in the Canadian Rockies and again at a place called Capreol in the Ontario farming belt. In Jasper the station was right in the town so we were able

*48. Bit chilly, dear*

to go and look at the shops in the main street even though it was rather chilly. It didn't take us long to realise that we were sharing the town with a heard of caribou. They seemed to be foraging for food – why they couldn't do that out in the wilds I don't know. Perhaps they got scraps from the train; who knows.

We were treated to some of the most amazing scenery I have ever seen on our train journey east towards Toronto. As first class passengers we had our own observation deck, a 360 degree enclosed panoramic viewing platform with swivel seats so we didn't have to miss a thing. At one point we passed a frozen lake; in fact it was not just the lake that was frozen but the waterfalls that fed into it too. All of a sudden there was an announcement over the Tannoy system saying that we should look out to our left. So we went up to our viewing area and saw a single deer being chased across the ice by about seven or eight wolves. The guy on the Tannoy said that you could do this trip year after year and never see such a sight; we felt very privileged.

One thing I noticed on the journey was that for miles and miles we would be travelling along a single track and then all of a sudden the train would join a dual track section where lo and behold a train would be coming in the opposite direction. Most of these were goods trains and they took for ever to pass us; they must have had fifty or sixty wagons apiece. By the time we stopped again in Capreol we had left the mountains behind us and had been travelling through mile after mile of flat arable plains, still covered in snow. Here there were dual tracks. I asked our steward why there were only single tracks through the mountains and he said it was due to constructional cost constraints. I have to say I didn't really understand this but then I'm not a civil engineer so what do I know!

We arrived in Toronto station mid evening and made our way to our hotel where we were staying for two nights before returning to good ol' Blighty. As we were getting off the train John Black came up to us and said, 'What are your plans whilst you're here in Toronto?' Well, Enid and I hadn't really given it much thought. We'd probably do what had worked for us throughout our trip and that was to ask for recommendations from the information desk in the hotel and I said as much to John.

'Well,' he said, 'if it's OK with you I'll give you a call this evening at your hotel.'

'Fine,' I said and didn't really give it much more thought. However true to his word John called at about 10:30 and told us that he had arranged for a car and driver to take us to Niagara Falls the next day. Well I consider

*49. Niagara Falls on the US side (left) and the Horseshoe Falls on Canadian side (right) from the Skylon Tower*

myself quite an intelligent bloke but it just hadn't registered with me that Niagara Falls was just outside Toronto and of course we couldn't leave without seeing that sight.

We had a great day out at Niagara Falls. Our driver-cum-guide was called Lee and he took us around the area and explained that it had now been designated a World Biosphere Reserve which sounded very impressive. As it was winter we more or less had the place to ourselves. We had a meal in the Skylon Tower revolving restaurant and were treated to some spectacular views of the falls.

When we got back we thought we'd do a bit of shopping. You might think that we would have to hop from one shop to the next in that cold but no, all the shops were in an underground mall: six miles of it. We didn't get cold but we didn't walk six miles either!

Now you may remember that as we started out on our journey my good friend Ron Mullings had taken us to the airport. Well, Ron had a brother, Bernard, who lived in Toronto. Bernard was an ex-sailor and frequently came over to attend Royal Naval Association functions and we had met him on a number of occasions both in the UK and indeed in Ireland. When

*50. Enid and me by Horseshoe Falls*

Enid and I got back to the hotel there was a message at reception saying that Bernard had called in at the hotel whist we were out. He had had to leave to make a hospital visit but the message said that we were obviously enjoying ourselves out on the town but if we got back at a reasonable time would we give him a call. So we called him and got hold of him and had a good chat. Unfortunately he lived sixty miles outside the city so it was too late to get together on this occasion.

And so we were on the final leg of our journey. We took a coach tour around the city and were very taken in by Toronto's famous landmark, Casa Loma. Built in 1911 by Sir Henry Pellatt, a Canadian financier, it is more like a castle with its ninety-eight rooms, crenulated towers, stable block and beautiful gardens set in five acres of ground. Unwise investments in WWI war bonds led to his bankruptcy and the eventual sale of the castle. Today our guide told us only two people live in it.

Our new acquaintance John Black had also said that we shouldn't worry about arranging a car to take us to the airport when we left; he'd send a truck round for us – a truck no less! I said we didn't have that many suitcases but he was insistent. As far as he was concerned we had to have amassed a fair amount of baggage from our travels and we were not to worry about transporting it to the airport. And you know, when we had all our luggage lined up in the hotel foyer waiting for this truck to arrive it did look quite a lot! As Enid and I stood there surveying all our chattels a voice was heard calling, 'Mr and Mrs Lawless!' We turned to find the smartest chauffeur you had ever seen standing there. We identified ourselves and he swiftly arranged for our luggage to be taken out to the truck. Well, I say truck; when we got outside it was a stretch limo. We'd never been so well looked after. What a way to end our trip! John Black was very kind to us and I wish now that we had remained in touch, so that we could have reciprocated should he have come to the UK.

We had been travelling for over fifty-two days without one single hiccup in our itinerary with RCI. Now, however, at the airport, just as we were heading home, a nice young stewardess informed us that the flight that we were scheduled to take to Amsterdam had been cancelled owing to a mechanical fault. Well, Friday 13 December may be unlucky for some but not for us! Almost immediately the same young lady came back and said that we were now booked on a direct flight to Heathrow which would arrive slightly earlier than the original flight had been scheduled to. I was able to call Ron Mullings to let him know about our flight change.

We had a wonderful Christmas recounting all our adventures to all our family and friends.

Our 'world trip' had been a truly remarkable adventure and something that we would always remember and be able to talk about for years and years to come. When I sat down to recollect the trip, however, I was full of trepidation. My memory is not what it used to be and I was afraid that I would miss out some important details. I shouldn't have worried because I found six lovingly crafted albums that Enid had compiled in a cupboard. We took twenty-seven rolls of film whilst we were away (which cost £127 to develop when we got back) and Enid had put all the photos in order with a little cryptic comments against each one, so it wasn't a trivial task. I guess she must have done this during one of my prolonged visits to Barnet General because I knew nothing about their existence.

We spent Christmas that year with Linda and Ian. It was whilst we were there that they told us they were splitting up. Enid was furious and strong words were exchanged about parental duty and such things. Enid was so angry that she told Ian that if he left Linda and the children then we would have nothing more to do with him.

It was obvious that the decision had already been made and sadly they did split up. A couple of years later, after the divorce came through, Ian was married again. To his credit he never forgot his fatherly duties, made sure the kids were OK and kept in contact with them.

# CHAPTER 22

# Associations

WHEN GRAHAM FIRST GOT married to Tina we were introduced to her parents, Pam and Herbie Cronk. Enid and I got on well with these two and we used to go out together a lot. We took them to golf club events at North Middlesex and to military do's too. We could often be found at officers' mess functions. Herbie was and still is a great chap and would as reciprocation take us to his Royal Naval Association (RNA) functions: the old comrades' association. Eventually he asked me if I would like to become a member of our local branch based in the British Legion located in Borehamwood. I of course said yes and so this is how Enid and I became members of the RNA too. We attended all the monthly meeting which we thoroughly enjoyed. Enid ran the 100 Club monthly lottery draw and shortly after we had joined I became the social secretary of a small but very enthusiastic committee. We organised a number of visits to other RNA Clubs and the occasional weekend visit and on one occasion we laid on a fortnight's holiday to Portugal. Thirty-two members and friends attended and all had a grand time; they are still talking about it. I rose through the ranks over a period of time to reach the dizzy heights of vice chairman but I had to resign from the committee altogether shortly afterward through my inability to attend all meetings owing to my continuing hospital stays and visits.

Because Borehamwood was close to us we always used to go to the Remembrance Day ceremony there. They would also always celebrate the Battle of Trafalgar and host a Christmas party. The RNA differs from the army and air force in the fact that they are national associations whereas the others are much more parochial. I guess that comes from the fact that there is just one navy whereas the army has its regiments and the air force its squadrons. Consequently we visited many different branches. When Enid and I were visiting relatives in South Yorkshire or Manchester, for example, we would often call in at the RNA branches there too.

That's how I spent a lot of my time but I have to say when I was fit I was spending as much time as I could golfing. Golf had become a major part of my life. I had held a number of prestigious positions in North

Middlesex Golf Club: Club Captain and President, and been granted honorary life membership. I am also a member of the Society of London Golf Captains and indeed I'm still on this society's committee today. I was president of the Foxes league too. I guess you could say that I'm gradually working my way through the ranks, as it were, but in a different organisation.

None of my health problems were going to prevent me from playing golf. The positions I held within the golf club and within the Society of London Captains enabled me to visit many clubs in the Home Counties and further afield. Indeed in 2002 I was asked to become Captain and Chairman of the Society of London Golf Captains, which was a great honour.

I took my responsibilities as Captain of the Society of London Captains very seriously and vowed to visit as many other Societies of Captains around the country as possible. And this I am proud to say I achieved.

Despite our ill health Enid and I were still able to have a holiday each year even if it were close to home: Ireland, Scotland or Isle of Man or indeed England. By this time Enid and I were getting fed up with flying. We were both suffering the after affects of our illnesses and walking was becoming a problem – not that we couldn't walk but that we couldn't walk very far. The distance from check-in to boarding in most airports was often beyond us, so we were going to places that we could drive to.

In 1998 however we decided for one last time to go to our timeshare apartment in Portugal and invite a couple – Charles and Anne Boulton – whom we were friendly with. They were a few years older than us and not as nimble, so we arranged with the travel authorities to have an assisted passage from check-in to the aeroplane plus reserved seats on the plane. Charles and Anne both had medical certificates that eased the way but when we arrived at the check-in desk there was a bit of a contretemps. The attendant at the desk refused to accept our hold baggage saying that we had already checked-in and handed in two suitcases. The Boultons were accepted and given their boarding passes but a supervisor had to be sent for to deal with us. After some considerable time the ground staff accepted that we couldn't be on the plane and standing in front of them as well. I produced the passports and we were given our boarding passes. We were all wondering who the other couple were who had caused all the confusion. We and the Boultons now got a buggy to the plane; we showed the air hostess our reserved seating tickets; and lo and behold two people were already occupying Enid's seat and mine. When the hostess enquired as to their names they replied that they were Mr and Mrs Lawless and what's more their initials were P and E: Peter and Ellen. To add to the coincidence, I knew the bloke; he had been a sergeant on the same recruiting course as me at Woolwich in 1970.

It was Enid's birthday on 12 February and I had ordered a bottle of champagne for the four of us to celebrate the occasion on the plane. This bottle had been given to Peter and Ellen but fortunately they hadn't opened it! The couple did have the good grace to swap seats so that our little party could sit together. I gave them each a glass of the bubbly.

If you think that the above is a coincidence, well, here's another: for the last twenty years or so Enid had been using the same hairdresser. About six years ago I also started to get my hair cut there. We became so friendly with the owners that we went out to dinner together on a number of occasions. They are called Tas and Nualla Stylianou. Both Tas's parents were Cypriots and had lived in a village in Cyprus which my Company (with me in it) had cordoned off and searched in 1957. The father was in the village at the time and remembered the searching of his house. We talked and laughed about it. But who would have thought it, eh; after fifty years, now *that's* a coincidence!

A little later in the year we were once again involved with the Boultons as they, Ann and Charles, had been invited to take part in the Kilroy show produced by the BBC. The subject was 'I love him but he's unfaithful'. The Boultons were asked if they knew of another couple that might fit the bill and they asked us if we would like to go with them. Both we couples were picked up by a stretch limo the day before the morning's broadcast to be taken through all the details and what would be expected of us. Next morning we were taken to the studio for the televised show and we became part of the live audience.

A number of couples admitted to having affairs and were put through the wringer by Kilroy after examining the whys and wherefores of these peccadillos, through questions and answers with the audience. He then asked if there was anyone in the audience who had stayed faithful throughout a long marriage, of say forty years or so. We had to have a show of hands – as previously arranged – and Kilroy upset Ann Boulton by picking me. He asked me how long I had been married and I told him forty-five years. He then asked what I thought of the cases we had just been discussing and I said that it wasn't my place to criticise anybody but what

I'd been listening to gave me a new meaning to the term 'playing around' which I'd always associated with golf. I continued by adding that in the case of a woman whose husband had freely admitted that he had had intercourse with some sixteen or seventeen different women, one of whom was his own daughter-in-law, I questioned her sanity as she still continued to live with him and forgave him. Kilroy then asked me what it was in my marriage that had stopped me looking elsewhere. I said I'd often looked but never touched and then explained that I believed in the marriage vows for one thing and the fact that I'd known my wife at infants' school at the age of five. We grew up together as friends; we liked each other's company; and after we were married we never went to bed on an argument. He then said, 'So Enid was your girlfriend at a very early age then.' I replied, 'Not likely; she was just another girl who couldn't play football.' Shortly afterwards Enid was asked to appear once again on the Kilroy Show which was about shopping for Christmas toys and entitled 'Dreading the cost of Christmas'. This she duly did and had plenty to say on the subject.

One of my good friends at North Middlesex Golf Club is Danny Hurley. Once we were holidaying in Ireland together with our wives. Danny, who had been looking for a property to purchase over there, found a four-bedroomed bungalow just outside the city of Kilkenny. We had stopped at a B&B there. Whilst talking in the B&B after supper the lady owner interrupted our conversation – had she heard correctly that we were looking for a house – if that was so she said there was a place just across from them that might be up for sale. So Danny, accompanied by nosey me, went to have a look with the lady, leaving the wives behind. As we were being shown around the place Danny fell in love with it. I went to fetch the women and they loved it too. Danny agreed with the owner to buy it and did so very quickly, and ever since people, family and friends have taken advantage of Danny's hospitality and had holidays there. Danny told Enid and me that we could use the bungalow whenever we wished, always assuming that his family, who of course had priority, weren't using it. We had some smashing times there. We made friends with the couple in the B&B, Betty and Dick McGrath, and there were times when Danny's friends were using the place and we would stay with Betty and Dick instead. When we did go to Ireland we always made time to visit my sister-in-law, my brother Jim's estranged wife Mary, who initially lived in Gorey in Co. Wexford but now lives in Dublin. She has a son James and daughters Siobhan, Ciara and Aoifa. James is married now to Ailish and they have two children Caoimhe and Niamh. Dear reader – wrap your tongues around those Gaelic names!

We often used to go to the bungalow and use it as a jumping off point to visit and explore almost all of Ireland, usually with our other good friends, Ron and Nora Mullings. On one trip Nora actually kissed the Blarney Stone – she's never stopped talking since. On another occasion we had our granddaughters with us, Sarah, Kelly and Emma who by this time were quite young ladies; Sarah was twenty and the other two in their late teens. One particular day, I remember, we decided to go to Blarney for the day. It was a hot summer day, not too common in Ireland, but it was early August and we were having a very nice spell of weather – thank you. We set off and had a short stop in Mitchelstown for a cold drink and carried on to Cork. When we arrived at the outskirts of the city we stopped at a set of traffic lights and one of the girls noticed steam coming from under the bonnet, so when the lights changed I parked and when I looked under the bonnet found even more steam. I checked the temperature gauge and it was in the red. Fortunately we still had some bottles of water so we poured these into the radiator – nearly scalding myself taking the cap off in the process – and after a while the engine cooled down.

In the meantime I went to find a garage and luckily found one, not too far from where we were, and asked them if they would contact the AA. They did this and asked for someone to come and have a look at the car. They gave us an ETA of thirty minutes but in fact a man arrived in ten. It was the top radiator hose that had split and caused the radiator to overheat. To cut a long story short, the car and passengers were towed to another garage and inspected (the car not the passengers) – and we were told that the garage didn't carry any spares for our car, they would have to get it from England. They told us we would have to stay overnight and they would arrange accommodation for us at a local hotel, where we were given two rooms. Now comes the interesting bit. None of us had any nightwear, nor any change of clothes or indeed any additional clothes. Enid and I had only sufficient medication for that day and nothing for the morrow. We agreed that we could manage until the next day, when we were assured that the car would be ready.

After breakfast the next morning I rang the garage. They said that the part had arrived but unfortunately it was the wrong size – they would have to send for another. We then tried to find a hire car but couldn't get one for we were told that both Enid and I were too old to get insurance and Sarah – the other driver – was too young. Stalemate! Enid and I had to get back to the bungalow in Kilkenny a.s.a.p. to get our medication. We eventually decided that we two would take a coach back to Kilkenny and the three girls, to keep each other company, would stay another night in the hotel. The garage was briefed on these arrangements. We set off on the coach and all the way back Enid was worrying about the girls, would they be all right.

I said, jokingly, 'They will probably be out on the town living it up.'

'Good God,' she said, 'what if something happens to them; we are responsible for them, they are under our care, you know.'

I explained that I had arranged with the girls that they were to stay in the hotel and ring us up at about 10 o'clock to let us know that they were OK. We got back all right and the girls rang; Sarah collected the car the next day and drove back to the bungalow – adventure over.

On another occasion we took Sarah and a Spanish friend of hers with us to Ireland. I should mention that Sarah had graduated from Chester University in Spanish with honours and was now working in Spain at a school teaching English to Spanish children. The Spanish girl was over on holiday. She really loved Ireland and enjoyed the various places we took her to, particularly the trip around the Ring of Kerry.

It did seem that our lives alternated between on the one hand, holidays and on the other, large periods of time in Barnet General Hospital. We always managed to turn the corner and get well again. At one time we were both in hospital at the same time. I suggested that we have a double bed but that didn't go down very well for some reason! However we did get put in adjoining wards; Enid in the women's ward and I in the men's, separated by only a partition.

Because we were never very sure about how our respective medical conditions were going to be and our decision about flying, we decided to give our time share apartment to Ian, having ascertained from Graham that he didn't want it and was happy for Ian to have it.

# CHAPTER 23

# To wrap up

IN THE LATTER PART OF Enid's life she suffered greatly from pain in her toes and feet. Not that she complained about this, even when she had to have numerous toes removed.

I would be lying if I said I wasn't worried about Enid or about myself; apart from dealing with the practicalities of Enid's diabetes I wasn't faring that well myself. I've thought long and hard as to what has been appropriate to include in this book because I'm sure, dear reader, that you did not want a blow by blow account of our increasingly poor health; after all this is not supposed to be a sick report. However by this time, our health was impacting on our lives and so I feel it must be mentioned here.

Luckily for me I had golf; golf was my saviour. I was able to continue playing even though an increasingly greater part of my lower joints was being replaced. In truth I think that getting out on the golf course was great therapy. Not only was it keeping me active on the course, I was becoming increasingly more involved in organising events off the course too.

In 2001 I accepted the position of Vice Captain and Chairman of the Society of London Golf Captains. I attended a few functions on behalf of the other officers of the Society that year including Derbyshire's dinner (which was held at the new football stadium), Manchester, Hertfordshire and Kent. This set me in good stead for my Captaincy. I don't mean to boast but the London Society of Golf Captains is recognised as one of the top societies in the country with every other Golf Captain's Society wanting to attend our annual dinner. Some of our previous Captains had not always been able to attend other counties' functions and I intended to go to every one.

So in 2002, I attended dinners in Edinburgh, Manchester, Liverpool, Derbyshire, Leicestershire and Cardiff, as well as all the local ones in the home counties: Hampshire, Sussex, Kent, Surrey, Essex, Oxfordshire, Hertfordshire. The only one I missed was Berkshire because it was the same night as the Hampshire function. Having decided to go to Hampshire's dinner my Vice Captain represented us at Berkshire. I might add that I put a few pounds on, with all those dinners.

One of these events was the Manchester Golf Captain's annual dinner in 2001, whilst I was still Vice Captain. I attended this dinner in the place of our Secretary who had been invited but couldn't go. I was sat next to the Manchester Vice Captain, a chap by the name of Billy Elliot (not the dancer!), and during our conversation it transpired that he knew of Harry and Greta Jones. Harry had served with me when I first joined up, you may remember, and was a regular in our group of old comrades who went to France each year to the D Day remembrance meetings and I was staying with him that night. Knowing that Billy would not have an official invitation to our coming annual dinner in London, I asked him if he would like to come as my personal guest. He of course was delighted because the London event had a reputation of being a dinner not to be missed. The following year, when we were both Captains, Billy invited me to come up the day before their annual dinner to stay over and play a game of golf with him. This I duly did and had a very enjoyable time. As the last year I stayed overnight with Harry and Greta.

That year, as Captain attending the more distant Captain's dinners for instance in Edinburgh, it wasn't possible for me to get there and back in a day, especially if the invitation included a round of golf too. When staying away I tried to look up as many old friends (like Harry and Greta) as I could and if they offered me a bed for the night that helped keep my expenses down. This meant that I spent a great deal of time away from home during the year. Although Enid never complained about my prolonged absences I know that she did mind but understood, as a true army wife, that these events were part of the job and well and truly stag.

In 2003 after I had passed on the mantle of Captain of the Society of London Captains I decided that the least I could do was treat Enid to a well deserved cruise. In fact we ended up doing two cruises back to back: two fourteen-day cruises. The first was a Mediterranean cruise where we flew to Rome and cruised the Greek Islands, into the Black Sea to Rumania and Odessa, finishing in Athens via Turkey. As we started the second phase of the cruise I became ill. Nobody had any idea what was the matter with me but I was unable to eat anything and so began to lose weight. The doctor asked if I wanted to be flown home but this would have spoilt things for Enid and therefore I said no, so the doctor confined me to bed. After four days I felt a bit better and so I was able to leave my cabin and although still poorly was able to join Enid on the rest of the cruise excursions. We visited Malta, Gibraltar, Casablanca, Lisbon, Vega, and Falmouth, finally disembarking in Southampton. I was then presented with a huge doctor's bill which fortunately I was able to claim back through our insurance.

Once we got home I went to see my own doctor who sent me off for some tests which resulted in me being hospitalised for three weeks whilst they tried to figure out what was wrong with me. By this time I had lost three stone in weight, fine for me when I was boxing but not at this age. They prodded and poked, scanned but still had no idea what the problem was. Finally they did a biopsy of my lungs and after the tests came back they announced that I had sarcoidosis. They explained that it was a disease that attacked the organs, particularly the lungs, and although there was no known cure it could be treated with steroids. The effect of the steroids was amazing; almost immediately I got my appetite back and I began to put weight back on. I got a feel-good factor and state of wellbeing. In fact it was so powerful that I woke up one morning to find for the first time in about ten years I was aroused. I said to Enid, jokingly, 'Come on, love, let's not waste this,' but by the time she remembered what to do, we'd missed our chance! A side effect was that I started to grow thick hair on my forearms.

After a while I realised that I had another problem. One day I would want to pee and couldn't and another I didn't feel that I wanted to pee but couldn't stop. Another visit to the hospital and more tests and another biopsy revealed that I had prostate cancer which had spread to the bladder. The oncologist told me that in view of my age and the treatment I was receiving for my sarcoidosis he wasn't sure that I could have a course of chemotherapy.

It was not the best of times and I was frightened about what the future might hold. Enid had lost her father and her brother to cancer and now she was upset by the thought of me going the same way. The urologist was fantastic; he sat Enid and I down and explained that all was not lost because although chemotherapy might not be a possibility surgery was an option. He could operate and remove my bladder and prostate and then by doing a series of other tests ensure that all the cancer had been removed. We should think about this carefully, as there were consequences and he looked at Enid as he said this. It would mean a urostomy bag and the possible end to our sex life. Well, at seventy-three years of age we both thought that the operation was a small price to pay for more happy years together, sex or no sex.

There is no doubt in my mind that those medical people saved my life. They got all the cancer and since then, touch wood, I have been cancer free. Yes I do have to go back for regular check-ups but I don't mind that. I can still play golf even though I now have a buggy to convey me between shots.

In 2005 North Middlesex Golf Club had its centenary and indeed the committee had been involved in preparing for this for several years. We had reminded the R&A of the fact and even got a mention on TV from Peter Alliss. We had had a number of fund raising activities including a golf competition counting down to 2005; it started in 2002 by being called centenary minus 3 and counted down each year to centenary zero in 2005. It was a great competition designed to involve all members, young and old. All our celebrations culminated in a grand ball in November where we had a massive marquee on the front car park. It really was a special occasion and everyone had a great time. A member – past Captain and good friend, John Dyke – wrote a book about the club's history over the last century, *North Middlesex Golf Club The First Hundred Years History 1905–2005* with which I like to think I helped.

In the autumn of 2007 I was told that I needed to have a triple heart bypass. I had the operation in November. It was successful and under normal circumstances I would have been released after two weeks. By now though Enid had been taken back into hospital with respiratory problems, so I was kept in for a further week.

Sadly Enid died on 3 December 2007. My only regret is that I was not able to see more of her before her final hours. She was diagnosed with MRSA whilst in hospital and because of my recent heart operation, it was considered by the doctors unwise for me to visit. At the time it never occurred to me that she wouldn't recover and be back home for Christmas but that wasn't to be.

Shortly before her death all the family – including me, now resolved to disobey my doctor's orders – were informed and called to the hospital so we were all by her side when she passed away.

# CHAPTER 24

# Afterthoughts

IN ALL HONESTY I HAD never considered that Enid would be the first to go. I had spent a great deal of time ensuring that she would be well provided for after I had gone. So it is strange now to be writing this memoir without her by my side although she is always there in my thoughts.

Out of the blue Bill Chevis phoned to tell me the sad news that Pat Montgomery had died. Pat had been our first Company Commander when we served together in Luneburg in 1948. Not only was I saddened by this but also Bill informed me that we were probably the only two surviving members of D Company under Pat's command. It just goes to show how time has passed. With this in mind he suggested that we attend the funeral which we did.

Whilst talking of Bill Chevis this reminds me of another incident in which he and I were involved. Whilst serving in Berlin the regiment had gone to winter training camp in Sennelager. As RQMS at the time I was left as the senior other rank back in Berlin. Bill was the 2IC of the regiment and stayed behind to command the rear party. As my superior officer he called me one day to say that he thought we should do an area inspection of the camp before the regiment returned. We were walking round and Bill said, 'Well, it all looks very clean,' to which I replied, 'Well, we don't know, do we?'

'What do you mean?' said Bill.

'Well it's all covered in too much snow, Sir,' I replied, 'and we don't know what's under it and we can't be shifting all this to find out!'

We kept on walking and Bill reflected, 'Do you remember when we first served together in Lüneburg and I was a platoon commander and you were a very young lance corporal?'

'Yes I do,' I replied.

'Here we are today, me second in command and you an RQMS. Did you ever think in those days that this is where we would be today?'

Without missing a beat, I said, 'Well, yes, I knew that I would but I had my doubts about you!'

'You always were a cheeky bugger,' Bill replied, and we had a good laugh. He and I remain friends and I'm sure that he still remembers that conversation.

Enid and I were in Christmas card contact for many years with Colonel David and Alice Wood. I learnt of David's passing through a member of the RNA who knew him. Having received details of his memorial service I discovered that it was on the same day as North Middlesex Golf Club's AGM. David's memorial service was in Devon but having been asked to second the proposal for the incoming President, John Penn, at the golf club I felt honour bound to attend both events but was not sure how I would achieve this. The drive to Devon was a four-hour journey each way but I worked it out – with military precision – that if I left home at 8:30 I could be in Devon by 12:30, attend the service and return to London in time for the start of the AGM. My plans worked beautifully and I even had time for a pie and a pint in the pub with the other officers before the service, as the church was next door. After the service I also had time to have a word or two with Alice before leaving, and got back in the nick of time for the AGM.

At the service I was acknowledged and respected as Major Peter Lawless, the retired army officer that rose up through the ranks, far removed from the scruffy little urchin from Brickfield Row, Rotherham, who could have so easily ended up being a miner like my father. Not that I'm ashamed of my heritage; it's just that I knew from the moment I stepped into a pair of army boots, that my destiny lay elsewhere.

I may have taken poetic licence in regards to my conversations with higher authorities, and the words might not be the same as those actually used but the gist of the matter is accurate.